Sweet on Denmark

Sweet on Denmark

CONTEMPORARY DANISH DESSERTS

Birthe Karen Jensen

Foreword by Ole Henriksen

In loving memory of my parents

Published in Australia in 2011 by
The Images Publishing Group Pty Ltd
ABN 89 059 734 431
6 Bastow Place, Mulgrave, Victoria 3170, Australia
Tel: +61 3 9561 5544 Fax: +61 3 9561 4860
books@imagespublishing.com
www.imagespublishing.com

Copyright © The Images Publishing Group Pty Ltd 2011
The Images Publishing Group Reference Number: 860

All rights reserved. Apart from any fair dealing for the purposes of private study, research, criticism or review as permitted under the Copyright Act, no part of this publication may be reproduced, stored in a retrieval system or transmitted in any form by any means, electronic, mechanical, photocopying, recording or otherwise, without the written permission of the publisher.

National Library of Australia Cataloguing-in-Publication entry:

Author:	Jensen, Birthe.
Title:	Sweet on Denmark / by Birthe Jensen.
ISBN:	9781864703504 (hbk.)
Subjects:	Desserts – Denmark.
	Cooking, Danish.

Dewey Number: 641.8609489

Production by The Graphic Image Studio Pty Ltd, Mulgrave, Australia
www.tgis.com.au

Pre-publishing services by Mission Productions Limited

Printed on 140 gsm GoldEast Matt art paper by Everbest Printing Co. Ltd. in Hong Kong/China

IMAGES has included on its website a page for special notices in relation to this and its other publications. Please visit www.imagespublishing.com.

Contents

10 Acknowledgments
12 Foreword
14 Preface
17 Advice before beginning
18 A history of Danish pastries

20 COPENHAGEN AND ZEALAND

22 Conditori & Café H.C. Andersen
Mette Søgaard, Confectioner

DANISH PASTRIES
Basic recipe 24
Snail *(Snegl)* 26
Cinnamon horn *(Kanelhorn)* 26
Chocolate bun *(Chokoladebolle)* 27
Spandauer 28

TRADITIONAL DANISH CREAM CAKES
Napoleon's hat *(Napoleonshat)* 29
Othello layer cake *(Othellolagkage)* 30
Sarah Bernhardt Cake *(Sarah Bernhardt)* 31
Goose breast *(Gåsebryst)* 32
Rubinstein cake *(Rubinsteinkage)* 33

34 Nilaus Bille Nielsen
Marzipan ring cakes *(Kransekage)* 36
Cold buttermilk soup *(Koldskål)* 37
Chocolate and raspberry truffles 37
Red fruit porridge *(Rødgrød)* with elderflower mousse 38
The cake of the year 2003 with beer 39

40 Saison
Erwin Lauterbach

Pears in boiled elderberries, yoghurt ice cream and nuts in vanilla 42
Soufflé pancakes with blueberries 43

44 Meyers
Claus Meyer

Rhubarb trifle 46
Bread 'n' butter pudding with rhubarb mash 47
Apple cake with syrup and cider 48
Apple soup with crisp apple rings 50
Drained junket with compote of mirabelle plums and toasted oats 51

52 **Le Sommelier**
Francis Cardenau

    Red fruit pudding with milk foam and almond ice cream 54

    Vanilla cream with poached blueberries and tarragon, and blood orange and passionfruit sorbet 55

    Warm chocolate ganache with mazarin, rhubarb and liquorice 56

58 **Restaurant Herman**
Thomas Herman Pedersen

    Bread layer cake (Brødtærte) 60

    21st-century raspberry canapé (Hindbærsnitte) 61

    French nougat with a taste of dream cake 62

    Red porridge flavoured marshmallow cream (Rødgrød med fløde som marshmallow) 62

    Inspiration of biscuit cake (Inspiration of kiksekage) 63

    Coffee bread from Fredericia (Kaffebrød som i Fredericia) 64

    Veiled farm girl (Bondepige med slør som smørrebrød) 65

66 **Søllerød Kro (Søllerød Inn)**
Jakob de Neergaard, Jan Restorff, Nicolas B Georg, Daniel Kruse

    Rhubarb with strawberries and almonds 68

    Apples, hazelnuts and herbs 69

    Raspberry, caramel and rosehips 70

    Passionfruit, cream chocolate and wood sorrel 71

72 FUNEN

74 **Falsled Kro (Falsled Inn)**
Randi Schmidt and Per Hallundbæk

    Sea buckthorn, carrots and crisp rye bread with liquorice 76

    Aromatic dessert with flowers from the garden at Falsled Inn 77

    Black September berries with hazelnuts 78

    Raspberries with sheep's milk, red pepper and peaches 79

80 SOUTHERN JUTLAND

82 **A history of Southern Jutland coffee and cakes**

84 **Fakkelgaarden**
Mikael Holm & Esben Krogh

    Blue cheese from Southern Jutland and rye bread, red onion rings, gel and cress 86

    Cheese with honey 87

Traditional bread layer cake from Southern Jutland 87
Apple cake 88
Juice blancmange with cream sauce and redcurrants 88
Spelt rice with lemon and cherries 89
Buttermilk mousse with fresh strawberries 90
Good advice *(Gode råd)* 91
Lard cakes *(Fedtkager)* 91
Jewish cakes *(Jødekager)* 91

92 Carl Christian Nissen
Fragilité 94
Dannebrog canapé *(Dannebrogsnitte)* 94
Gallop pretzel *(Galopkringle)* 95

96 MID JUTLAND

98 Restaurant Frederikshøj
Palle Enevoldsen & Wassim Hallal
Apple with chocolate cake 100
Coffee and mascarpone cake 102
Strawberry and orange cake 103
Cherries and chocolate cake 104

106 NORTHERN JUTLAND

108 Ruths Restaurant, Skagen
Michel Michaud
Fruit salad of rosehips and oranges 110
Poor knights *(Arme riddere)* 111

DANISH WINES
114 The Danish wine industry

120 Facts about Denmark

APPENDIX
124 Conversions and standard measurements

126 Glossary

127 Useful addresses

128 References

129 Index by recipe name

130 Index by category

132 Photography credits

Acknowledgments

PUTTING TOGETHER *SWEET ON DENMARK* has been a delicious, mouth-watering journey through a whole new world of exciting taste sensations. Over the past year I have met many confectioners and chefs who have inspired me while writing this book. Thank you so much to the following people, who not only shared their great knowledge, but also very generously provided me with recipes for this book: Mette Søgaard, Nilaus Bille Nielsen, Claus Meyer, Francis Cardenau, Erwin Lauterbach, Thomas Herman Pedersen, Jakob de Neergaard, Jan Restorff, Daniel Kruse, Nicolas B. Georg, Randi and Per Hallundbæk, Mikael Holm, Esben Krogh, Palle Enevoldsen, Wassim Hallal and Michel Michaud. Also, thank you to Mette Rahbek Jensen and Thomas Koch from Meyers, Linda Bengtson from Saison, Peter Brinks and Jesper Dyrvig-Pedersen from Fakkelgaarden, and Jan Ludvigsen and Peter Bøgil from Ruths Hotel & Strandhotellet in Skagen for photography as well as assistance.

Historian Ms Bi Skaarup and historian/curator Dr Inge Adriansen from the Sønderborg Castle Museum of Southern Jutland possess an enormous amount of knowledge and I am grateful for their assistance with historical information about the history of Danish pastries and the cakes of Southern Jutland respectively.

It was a great pleasure to meet Mr Sven Moesgaard at his award-winning winery in Dons in the Danish wine region of Jutland. He introduced me to the grape varieties thriving in Denmark and the secrets behind his success today.

Without Danish photographer Mr Flemming Nissen this book would not have been the same. He tirelessly travelled across the country photographing these delicious desserts, which I am grateful for. Thanks also to Lars Gundersen for the photo of the team from Søllerød Kro, to Tellus Works for the photos of Claus Meyer and his desserts, to Lars Lind for the photos of the cake of the year and chocolate and raspberry truffles from Nilaus Bille Nielsen, and to Tivoli, Hans Peder Sølvbjerg, Casper Depka Carstens, Line Kornbeck-Mørup, Pernille Bech Jørgensen from Landbrug & Fødevarer and Visit Aarhus, who all provided me with photos for the book. A big thank you to the great team at Images Publishing who patiently put this book together and supported me in every way: Alessina Brooks, Paul Latham, Beth Browne and Joe Boschetti.

Ole Henriksen kindly provided the foreword for which I am very grateful. Thank you, Ole, for your passion and inspiration. Finally, thank you to anyone who reads this book. I hope that it will be an inspiration to all who wish to know about Danish cuisine or visit this beautiful country.

Foreword

Ole Henriksen is a highly acclaimed Danish skin care specialist. His beauty salon Ole Henriksen Face/Body Spa is located in Sunset Boulevard in Los Angeles. His remarkably effective complexion treatments work their magic on some of the world's most famous faces. Henriksen has published a number of bestselling books and has worked as a motivational speaker and presenter for many television programs and wellness seminars. Born and raised in the small town of Nibe in Northern Jutland, Denmark, Henriksen is known for his enthusiasm, cheerfulness and his warm and inspiring personality.

WHO DOESN'T ENJOY the beautiful ritual of sipping coffee or tea from a delicate cup, and biting into a delicious dessert elegantly presented on a fine piece of china? Great desserts are like fine wines, a treat to the palate created from a melody of sumptuous textures and distinct flavours. So how can a book featuring dessert recipes by Denmark's top confectioners and chefs be anything but a mouth-watering experience?

Birthe Jensen's magnificent book combines the best of simple and uncomplicated desserts with more artistic creations that I will take the liberty of labelling the 'haute couture' of desserts. Each chef featured clearly loves the art of what they do, having perfected their craft with passion and creativity over the years. The foundation, or essence, of a great dessert, we learn from the masters, is based on using ingredients of the highest quality. So it is reassuring to know that many richly textured desserts are bursting with antioxidants and other important nutrients in addition to tasting delicious.

I love the fact that each recipe presented in *Sweet on Denmark* is easy to follow, especially for an unseasoned pastry chef like myself. Indeed, how could I be given the great honour of writing the foreword without testing several of the recipes? So my spouse Laurence and I went shopping for our supplies and got our baking gear out, and made the deliciously decadent Othello Layer Cake for a dinner party at our house. It was received with applause by our guests. Encouraged by the warm reception our next creation became Napoleon's Hat, because we both love marzipan and dark chocolate. So we are on a roll now and loving every minute of it. Next on my list to try is something more simple, my favourite childhood summer indulgence Cold Buttermilk Soup with *Kammerjunkere*. I remember how my brothers and I would fight over my mother's home-baked *Kammerjunkere*, crunchy and sweet as they were. It is wonderful and comforting to be reminded how some of our favourite desserts represent more than a delicious treat, by having so many sweet memories associated with them.

Here is a toast to everyone's sweet memories and to Birthe Jensen for sharing *Sweet on Denmark* with the world.

Ole Henriksen

Preface

JUST AS THE FRENCH HAVE CAMEMBERT, the Italians pasta and the Germans sauerkraut, the Danes have pastries in many styles and shapes, and with countless varieties of fillings. Danish pastry is Denmark's major contribution to international culinary culture, so much so that 'Danish' has become another word for this style of pastry in some parts of the world. This is particularly common in the US, whereas in the UK it is known as Danish pastry and in Austria as *Dänische plunder* or *Kopenhagener gebäck*.

The Danes enjoy myriad confectioneries and fresh produce available throughout the country. They love to celebrate every occasion, the 'big moments in life', and very often the meal is only considered complete after a cake, pastry or dessert has been served. There is always an excuse to enjoy life.

This book offers a taste of the local Danish pastries, traditional cakes and delicious desserts, with recipes to be made and enjoyed at home.

Danish cuisine has been embraced by a new generation of confectioners and chefs on the cutting edge of innovative and creative cooking, while still respecting and maintaining Danish culinary traditions. There are 12 Michelin-star restaurants in Copenhagen, which is more than in any other city in Scandinavia. Danish cuisine has changed over the past decade as a result of European influences and, given the abundance of Denmark's excellent produce for each season, such as fruit and vegetables, dishes are very often based on organic produce. Indeed, the Danes are demonstrating an increased focus on health and food quality in order to protect themselves and the environment. Many products from small organic producers can now be found on supermarket shelves among produce from the larger food companies.

Denmark has shifting seasons and changing weather patterns, warm coasts and long summer days with many hours of sunshine, which guarantees a bountiful harvest of fruit and vegetables blessed with fantastic structure and taste.

This book presents some of the best Danish confectioners and chefs from various regions of Denmark. The desserts were selected by the chefs themselves and each recipe shows Danish produce at its best, from local creamy cheese and ice cream to traditional Danish fruit, such as deliciously juicy apples and strawberries. Some of the chefs were born in France or Lebanon, but they have lived in Denmark for numerous years, interpreting

Preface (continued)

local tradition and food culture at its best. The success of these chefs and confectioners is directly related to their personalities, passion, love of their art and sheer hard work, and I am grateful to be able to pass on their recipes.

I have lived most of my life in other countries, but every time I visit Denmark it is always a great joy to see, smell and taste the characteristics of the seasons that remind me of my childhood: Denmark's spring, beech trees sprouting leaves, sweet apples, plums, blackberries, strawberries, sour cherries and new sweet potatoes. I never tire of freshly baked pastries directly from the baker on a Sunday morning, the crisp rye bread, traditional cakes and red fruit pudding with cream on warm summer evenings.

I grew up on the Island of Als in the far south of Denmark, which remains a very special place for me.

This book includes a chapter about the cakes of Southern Jutland, which originated at the beginning of the 20th century and are well known throughout Denmark.

Since 2000, Denmark has been an officially recognised wine producer on the international wine scene, winning silver and gold medals in competition with winemakers from France and Italy. This book provides an overview of Danish winemaking and a portrait of one of the most successful makers of sweet wine in Denmark.

It is my hope that this book will excite your taste buds and prove to be an inspiration and source of enjoyment for many years. Alternatively, just sit back, relax and enjoy vicariously the amazing photos of these Danish delights.

Birthe Karen Jensen

Advice before beginning

- Read each recipe from start to finish to ascertain if you have all the necessary ingredients and equipment on hand. Sometimes you will need to prepare part of a recipe one or two days before serving.

- After you have read the recipe, gather all the required ingredients and equipment.

- Both metric and imperial measurements are provided in these recipes. It is advisable to use a measuring utensil when a recipe calls for a tablespoon or teaspoon.

- A confectionery/jam thermometer is required for many of the recipes in this book.

- An ice cream machine is used in many recipes in this book. As an alternative, you can also freeze the sorbet and stir every 30 minutes until the texture is smooth.

- When a recipe calls for butter it can be either unsalted or salted.

- When a recipe calls for flour it can be plain white (all-purpose) flour.

- Weigh ingredients before starting.

- It is important to preheat the oven before baking. Most ovens take about 10 minutes to reach the required temperature.

- Use the middle of the oven when baking.

- Ovens do vary so check the cake to see if it is ready before removing from the oven. Stick a clean toothpick into the cake near the centre and remove it. There should not be any batter or wetness on the toothpick.

- All recipes serve four people unless otherwise stated.

> *American Danish can be doughy, heavy, sticky, tasting of prunes and is usually wrapped in cellophane. Danish Danish is light, crisp, buttery and often tastes of marzipan or raisins; it is seldom wrapped in anything but loving care.*
>
> R. W. Apple Jr., 'The Danish Worth an Ocean Voyage',
> *The New York Times*, 22 November, 1978

A history of Danish pastries

DANISH PASTRIES HAVE EVOLVED over nearly 200 years to become an art form that is unique to Denmark. Early Danish confectioners learned their skills from Austrian and Swiss confectioners, and then developed their own style to suit the Danes.

It all began in Copenhagen in 1837 when a young businessman, Niels Christian Albeck, bought a property in Købmagergade, part of which was a bakery. Two years later he was given dispensation to become a trainee confectioner and in 1845 he decided to go on an educational tour to Vienna. During his stay he organised for three trainee confectioners to return with him to Denmark and with their help he established the first Danish 'Vienna bakery' and received permission from the magistrate of Copenhagen to bake pastries.

His bakery became well known and following his success many other bakers applied to open Vienna bakeries, as noted in the city archive of Copenhagen.

The dough is characterised by the use of roll-in fat (a type of margarine), which was incorporated from the 18th century, to create a flaky texture. The use of yeast was a later development, as seen in cookery books from the early 19th century.

The pastries became a great success in Denmark, among other *plundergebäcken*, which are made from a sweet piece of sweet yeast dough that is wrapped in butter and folded several times. The result was a masterpiece of pastry that was very light, crisp and delicate. The Danish confectioners soon adjusted and improved the recipes and developed many different types of Danish pastries, including *basser*, *snegl* and *spandauer*.

Many Danish specialities were created by Copenhagen confectioners in the years between 1870 and 1911 including raspberry canapé (*hindbærsnitte*), goose breast (*gåsebryst*) and the Sarah Bernhardt among others. There has been a long tradition of naming cakes after people or events. Cakes have also been named after famous operas and even a general: the Othello layer cake (*Othellolagkage*) and Napoleon's hat (*Napoleonshatte*) respectively. It also became become popular to give Danish confections names originating from geography, history, literature, music and the dramatic arts, which have since become legendary. Some creative confectioners created cakes to resemble castles and other well-known buildings.

During this time, it was necessary for members of the privileged bourgeoisie to make a good impression among their peers, so they served the latest innovative cakes from the Swiss or Viennese confectioneries as they were called then. Women would meet at these confectioneries in the afternoon to have a chat and to enjoy cakes and pastries, coffee, tea, chocolate and spirits.

Copenhagen and Zealand

danish pastry

Today there are approximately 100 types of Danish pastries with a variety of fillings.

Conditori & Café H.C. Andersen

" *My intentions are to create Danish pastries where quality and accuracy, the cornerstones of production, are combined with traditional and modern confectionery art and a consistently high level of customer service* "

Mette Søgaard

CONDITORI & CAFÉ H.C. ANDERSEN is situated in the centre of Copenhagen near the town hall and the statue of its namesake, Danish poet and storyteller Hans Christian Andersen.

The café's present owner, Mette Søgaard, has made a significant impact on the confectionery industry of Denmark. In 2009 she received the industry's highest award – the Order of St. Honoré. It is an international award for confectioners of an exceptionally high standard who have made a significant contribution to the art of confectionery. Throughout her career Søgaard has mentored 25 trainees, many of whom have received awards. She has also won prestigious awards such as 'Dessert of the year' and 'Cake of the year' and contributed to creating the wedding cake for Crown Prince Frederik and Crown Princess Mary of Denmark in 2004.

At Conditori & Café H.C. Andersen one can enjoy coffee, pastries, cakes and chocolate as well as lunch. Søgaard's recipes demonstrate an emphasis on quality and the use of first-class raw ingredients. Customers can watch the cakes being made through an open kitchen. The pastries, cakes, tarts, layer cakes and desserts, among others, are all based on traditional recipes. The team strives to provide customers with the best service and quality while still being innovative. 'The service is very important and the atmosphere is cosy in both the café and shop. It is important that my employees and colleagues show enthusiasm, responsibility, flexibility and endurance', Søgaard says. 'The urge for new adventures is the recipe for success and should be the goal for each staff member', she adds. Among Søgaard's 27 employees is her son, Morten Alling Søgaard, who has also won several awards for his innovative cakes.

Søgaard considers education of new confectioners paramount and for 22 years she has been working as an examiner for confectionery education at the National School of Bakery and Confectionery in Denmark as well as being chairwoman of the school's council. She is also part of the interdisciplinary committee between schools and the Danish Ministry of Education, which was established to develop and maintain the educational programme based on regulations set out by the Ministry.

Søgaard has owned Conditori & Café H.C. Andersen since 1984. After earning her degree as a confectioner in 1978 she worked with many confectioners in Copenhagen, gaining considerable experience. In 1980, at the age of 22, she owned her own confectionery. Since 1984 Søgaard has served delicious traditional pastries as well as innovative new cakes in her cosy café and confectionery in the heart of Copenhagen.

Danish pastries

Basic recipe

250 ml (8 fl oz) milk
15 g (½ oz) yeast
1 egg, whipped
35 g (1 oz) sugar
1½ tsp salt
3 tsp ground cardamom
500 g (16 oz/1 lb) plain wheat flour
100 g (4 oz) cold butter
150 g (5 oz) softened butter for wrapping

Utensils: bowls, saucepan, mixer, rolling pin, spatula

In a bowl, whip the egg. Pour some of the milk into a saucepan and warm over medium heat. Dissolve the yeast in the warm milk. Add the rest of the milk and the whipped egg. In a separate bowl, mix together sugar, salt, ground cardamom, flour and butter. Add the combined dry ingredients carefully into the yeast and milk mixture. Blend it all carefully in a food processor or a mixer, so that the end result is a smooth and soft dough. Let the dough rest in a refrigerator or a cool place for 15 minutes.

On a floured bench or table, gently roll out the dough into a long rectangle about 5 millimetres (⅛ inch) thick. Use a spatula to lightly cover half of the dough's surface with butter, fold the other half over and roll out the dough again. The dough needs to rest for 10 minutes in the refrigerator between each rolling out, otherwise the butter will run and the dough will shrink too much. Repeat this procedure many times, as shown in the photographs, until all the butter has been used.

Following are four of the most popular pastries in Denmark – each containing a different filling.

danish pastries

Danish Wienerbrød has a flaky or crumbly texture and can be made in many styles and with various fillings, such as almonds, chocolate, jam, macaroon or marzipan.

When making the pastry, take care to blend the fat (butter) and flour thoroughly before adding any liquid. When mixing, ensure that the pastry doesn't toughen.

Start by making the basic recipe and then choose the style and filling you want for each pastry.

Snail (Snegl)

100 g (4 oz) sugar

100 g (4 oz) margarine

20 g (¾ oz) ground cinnamon

Glazing
1 egg, lightly whipped

White icing glaze
100 g (3 oz) powdered sugar or icing sugar

approximately 1 tbsp boiling water

Filling: Cinnamon remonce

Cinnamon remonce
Utensils: Mixer, rolling pin, spatula, baking tray, baking paper, pastry brush

Carefully blend sugar, cinnamon and half of the margarine in a mixer. Gradually add the rest of the margarine. Keep mixing until all lumps have disappeared.

On a floured bench or table, roll out the dough so that it measures approximately 20 by 45 centimetres. Then use a spatula to spread the remonce across the dough. Roll the dough lengthwise, so that it becomes a long sausage. Then cut slices measuring 3 centimetres. Place the slices on a baking tray lined with baking paper. Ensure there is some space between the slices. Place the tray in a warm place and let it rise for an hour. Glaze the slices with a whipped egg. Place in a preheated oven at 200 °C (390 °F) for approximately 15 minutes. When cold, use a spatula that has been dipped in warm water to add white icing glaze to the middle of the snail.

White icing glaze
Blend icing sugar and water.

Cinnamon horn (Kanelhorn)

This speciality is not a traditional pastry, but it is very popular among the Danes and sold throughout Denmark.

1.2 l (2 pt/7 fl oz) full-cream milk

400 ml (13 fl oz) fresh cream

190 g (7 oz) sugar

175 g (6 oz) cornflour

1 vanilla pod

200 g (7 oz) pasteurised egg yolks

Glazing
1 egg, lightly whipped

Filling: Cinnamon remonce (see Snail recipe above for ingredients) and vanilla cream

Vanilla cream
Utensils: saucepan, bowl, knife, rolling pin, baking tray, baking paper, pastry brush

Make cinnamon remonce according to the instructions in the Snail recipe above.

For the vanilla cream, combine the seeds from the vanilla pod, milk and cream and bring to the boil. In a bowl, blend sugar, cornflour and egg yolks. When the milk begins to boil take it off the heat, then add the egg mixture and whip it all until it becomes a soft mass. Pour the cream in a bowl and put it in a cold place until it has settled.

On a floured bench or table roll out the dough, until it measures 30 by 45 centimetres. Cut three 10-centimetre slices lengthwise. Then, cut each slice into 6 triangles. Place them on a tray lined with baking paper. Place a small drop of vanilla cream and remonce on the wide side of the triangles. Roll the triangles from the top point to the opposite (wide) edge so that they look like horns.

Set aside the baking tray in a warm place and let the dough rise for an hour.

Use a pastry brush to glaze the pastries with the whipped egg. Bake in a preheated oven at 200 °C (390 °F) for approximately 15 minutes.

Chocolate bun
(Chokoladebolle)

Glazing
1 egg, lightly whipped

Cocoa icing
100 g (4 oz) powdered sugar or icing sugar

approximately 1–2 tbsp cocoa powder

approximately 1 tbsp boiling water

Filling: Vanilla cream (see Cinnamon horn recipe opposite for ingredients)

For decoration: Cocoa icing

Utensils: bowl, rolling pin, baking tray, pastry brush

Make vanilla cream according to the instructions in the Cinnamon horn recipe opposite.

On a floured bench or table, roll out the dough, so that it measures 30 by 40 centimetres. Cut 12 10-centimetre squares.

Place a small dot of cream on the middle of each square and fold in each tip so that they meet in the middle. Turn the buns upside down and place them on a baking tray lined with baking paper. Put the tray in a warm place and let them rise for an hour. Glaze with a whipped egg. Bake in a preheated oven at 200 °C (390 °F) for approximately 15 minutes.

Glaze the tops of the buns with cocoa icing.

Cocoa icing
Blend icing sugar, cocoa powder and water.

Spandauer

100 g (4 oz) marzipan
100 g (4 oz) sugar
100 g (4 oz) softened butter

Glazing
1 egg, lightly whipped

Filling: Borgmester and vanilla cream (see Cinnamon horn recipe on page 26 for ingredients)

Utensils: bowl, food mixer, baking tray, baking paper, pastry brush

Make vanilla cream according to the instructions in the Cinnamon horn recipe on page 26.

For the borgmester gently blend the marzipan, sugar and half the butter in a food mixer. Gradually add the rest of the butter. Mix well until there are no lumps.

On a floured bench or table, roll out the dough so that it measures 30 by 40 centimetres. Cut 12 squares measuring 10 by 10 centimetres.

Place a small amount of the borgmester mixture on the middle of each pastry and fold all corners so that they meet in the middle. Make a small hollow or dent in the centre of the pastry. Squeeze a drop of vanilla cream in the middle of each pastry and place the pastries on a baking tray lined with baking paper. Set aside the tray in a warm place and let the pastries rise for an hour before glazing them with the whipped egg. Bake in a preheated oven at 200 °C (390 °F) for approximately 15 minutes. Cool before serving.

To decorate
Spandauer can be topped with chopped almonds or other nuts.

Traditional Danish cream cakes

Napoleon's hat
(Napoleonshat)

Filling
240 g (8 oz) sugar

500 ml (16 fl oz/1 pt) pasteurised egg whites

700 g (25 oz) marzipan

Sweet pastry
450 g (1 lb) flour

300 g (10 oz) butter

150 g (5 oz) icing sugar

1 egg

Decoration
100 g (4 oz) dark chocolate (for example Valrhona Caraque, which has a mild round taste with a hint of berries)

Filling
Utensils: saucepan, bowl, spoon

Warm egg whites and sugar over a hot water bath, ensuring the temperature does not exceed 50 °C (120 °F). Then, combine with the marzipan.

Sweet pastry
Utensils: bowl, spoon, 12-centimetre circle cutter or a glass of equivalent size, baking tray, baking paper, saucepan, dish

Lightly knead all ingredients together. On a floured bench or table, roll out the dough to a thickness of 3 millimetres and cut out small circles measuring 12 centimetres in diameter. Use a glass if you don't have a 12-centimetre circle cutter. Roll 25-gram (1 oz) balls of the marzipan mixture and place them in the middle of the circles. Then bend three sides of the dough across the marzipan ball, so that it looks like a hat. Bake the cakes on a tray lined with baking paper in a preheated oven at 180 °C (350 °F) for approximately 12 to 15 minutes until lightly golden. Allow cakes to cool.

Decoration
In a saucepan melt the chocolate, then dip the bases of the pastries in the chocolate and place them on a dish.

Napoleon's hat, named after the French Emperor, has been a popular cake for decades. The small cake is normally shaped in a triangle like a traditional emperor's hat and consists of dough filled with marzipan and decorated with dark chocolate.

Othello layer cake
(Othellolagkage)

The cake is named after Guiseppe Verdi's 1887 opera Otello, which was based on Shakespeare's tragedy Othello. The opera was first performed in Denmark at the Royal Theatre in 1898.

250 g (8 oz) butter

300 g (10 oz) icing sugar

300 ml (10 fl oz/½ pt) eggs

300 g (10 oz) flour

10 g (2 pinches) baking powder

Cocoa icing
100 g (4 oz) powdered sugar or icing sugar

approximately 1–2 tbsp cocoa powder

approximately 1 tbsp boiling water

Vanilla cream
Make vanilla cream according to the instructions in the Cinnamon horn recipe on page 26.

Whipped cake layers
Utensils: bowl, mixer, 3 baking trays, baking paper, rolling pin, spatula, piping bag

Blend the butter and icing sugar for approximately 10 minutes. Add one third of the eggs gradually, add flour and baking powder and finally add the remaining two thirds of the eggs gradually. Mix thoroughly until there are no lumps. Line three baking trays with baking paper. Separate the cake mixture in three portions and place a third on each of the baking trays. Roll out the mixture so that each layer measures 25 centimetres in diameter. Bake the cake layers in a preheated oven at 180 °C (350 °F) for approximately 10 minutes until lightly golden.

To assemble
Spread the vanilla cream on one cake layer and repeat for another two layers. Use a piping bag to cover the edges with the cream or, alternatively, use marzipan to cover the edges.

To decorate
Top the cake with cocoa icing.

Cocoa icing
Blend icing sugar, cocoa powder and water.

Tip: You can add macaroons to the whipped layer cake mixture and/or add 35 grams (1 oz) of almonds with the vanilla cream.

Sarah Bernhardt Cake
(Sarah Bernhardt)

400 g (14 oz) dark chocolate

1 l (2 pt) full cream

150 g dark chocolate (for decoration)

Macaroons

200 g (7 oz) marzipan

400 g (14 oz) sugar

100 ml (4 fl oz) pasteurised egg whites

Sarah Bernhardt cream
Note: Start the day before.
Utensils: bowl, saucepan, whisk, cling film, spoon

Melt the chocolate in a bowl over a hot water bath. Warm the cream to its boiling point, and then whisk it into the melted chocolate until homogenous. Wrap tightly in cling film and refrigerate until the following day. The following day, whip the mixture lightly, so it becomes firmer, but make sure that it does not separate.

Macaroons
Utensils: whisk, piping bag, baking tray, baking paper

Whisk the marzipan and sugar until there are no lumps, and then add the egg whites gradually. Use a piping bag to form 15 macaroons. Place them on a baking tray lined with baking paper. Bake in a preheated oven at 180 °C (350 °F) for minimum of 20 minutes. It is important that the oven is not opened until the last minute; otherwise the macaroons will collapse.

Once cooked, the macaroons should weigh approximately 30 grams (1 oz) each.

Cover the cakes with the chocolate cream.

Tip: You can also use candied/crystallised violets for decoration.

This cake was created by a confectioner named Steen in Amager, a suburb of Copenhagen. Feted French actress Sarah Bernhardt (1844–1923) visited Denmark for the first time in 1880. In 1911 she was honoured with a cake in her name when she visited the city for the fourth time and spoke of her memories Danish. The cake still exists and can be bought in almost all bakeries in Denmark. It consists of a macaroon layer with chocolate cream or mousse covered with dark chocolate.

Goose breast (Gåsebryst)

Gåsebryst is one of the few cakes created outside Copenhagen in Næstved or Slagelse. It is made of a layer of pastry with prune marmalade, vanilla cream (see Cinnamon horn recipe on page 26 for ingredients) and whipped cream.

250 g (8 oz) high-quality butter puff pastry

Prune marmalade
1 kg (2 lb) prunes
200 ml (7 fl oz) water
350 g (12 oz) sugar
10 g (⅓ oz) pectin
Seeds from ½ vanilla pod

Decoration
300 g (10 oz) marzipan
250 g (8 oz) double cream, whipped
Icing sugar, for rolling out

Pastry
Roll out the puff pastry, so that it measures 12 by 30 centimetres and prick it with a fork to avoid bubbles. Bake on a tray lined with baking paper in a preheated oven at 180 °C (350 °F) for about 15–20 minutes, until golden and crisp.

Prune marmalade
Utensils: knife, saucepan, spoon, bowl

Split, pit and chop the prunes into small pieces. Bring water to the boil, add prunes and vanilla seeds and boil, covered, for 5 minutes. Combine the sugar and pectin and pour it gradually into the boiling marmalade. If possible, pour the marmalade into a heat-sterilised glass bowl, which will prolong its shelf life, then set aside in a cool place.

Decoration
Make vanilla cream according to the instructions in the Cinnamon horn recipe on page 26.

Utensils: spatula, mixer, piping bag, rolling pin, knife

If the pastry has changed shape while baking, trim the sides so that it is straight. Spread with an even layer of prune marmalade. Blend the vanilla cream with a little whipped cream, so that it becomes light and airy. Place the cream in a piping bag and spray it on top of the prune marmalade. Then add whipped cream to form a pyramid measuring approximately 7 centimetres.

Roll out the marzipan, using icing sugar to avoid it sticking to the work surface. When it measures 30 by 15 centimetres, place the marzipan carefully across the cake and cut it to shape. With a sharp knife cut the cakes into sizeable pieces (approximately 5–6 centimetres).

To decorate
Sprinkle cocoa on top of the cake.

Rubinstein cake (Rubinsteinkage)

100 g (4 oz) almonds

2 egg whites

100 g (4 oz) sugar

1 tsp baking powder

Fromage

650 g (23 oz) cream

100 g (4 oz) pasteurised egg yolks

150 g (5 oz) icing sugar

9 gelatine leaves

100 ml (4 fl oz) rum (reserve some of the rum for sprinkling between layers)

Wales (vandbakkelser)

200 ml (7 fl oz) water

100 g (4 oz) butter

100 g (4 oz) plain flour

200 ml (7 fl oz) eggs

Decoration

150 g (5 oz) dark chocolate

50 ml (1⅔ fl oz) raspberry jam

Macaroon layer
Utensils: saucepan, whisk, baking tray, baking paper, piping bag

Blanch the almonds by placing them in a saucepan, adding enough water to cover the almonds. Bring to the boil. Let the almonds stand in the hot water for a maximum of 1 minute, then rinse under cold water and drain. Allow to dry before sliding their skins off. Chop the almonds finely.

With a whisk, whip the egg whites until very stiff, then add the almonds, sugar and baking powder. Line a 22-centimetre baking tray with baking paper. Use a piping bag to pipe macaroons onto the tray. Bake the macaroons in a preheated oven at 180 °C (350 °F) for a minimum of 20 minutes. It is important that the oven is not opened until the last minute; otherwise the macaroons will collapse.

Fromage
Utensils: 3 bowls, whisk

In one bowl, whip the cream. In another bowl, whisk the egg yolks with the icing sugar and blend this mixture into the whipped cream. Soak the gelatine in cold water for approximately 5 minutes or until it is softened, squeeze the excess water, then mix it into the rum until dissolved. Then, whisk this mixture into the cream.

Wales (Vandbakkelser)
Utensils: casserole dish, whisk, piping bag, baking tray, baking paper

In a casserole dish, bring water and butter to the boil. Add the flour and mix well. Add the eggs one at a time and mix until smooth. Use a piping bag to pipe the mixture into small pyramid shapes. Place them on a baking tray lined with baking paper. Bake the cakes at 220 °C (450 °F) in a preheated oven for approximately 10 minutes until they are lightly golden. It is important that the oven is not opened until the last minute; otherwise the cakes will collapse.

Decoration
Sprinkle the macaroon layer with a little of the reserved rum, then spread raspberry marmalade over the top and add the fromage mixture. Decorate the wales by dipping them in warm chocolate that has been melted over a hot water bath. Place the wales around the cake as decoration.

Tip: You can also use nougat to decorate the cake.

This cake was named after a famous piano virtuoso, Anton Rubinstein (1829–1894), when he visited Copenhagen in the middle of the 19th century. It is one of the most popular cakes in Denmark, but its creator is unknown. The cake represents a piano with white and black keys. Anton Rubinstein visited Denmark many times and became friends with the Danish author and storyteller Hans Christian Andersen (1805–1875).

Nilaus Bille Nielsen

> *" I like to keep the sweet kitchen simple, meaning that I like to get the best out of the ingredients, and not change the dish so that it becomes unrecognisable. I think it is important to use the seasonal ingredients that surround us "*
>
> Nilaus Bille Nielsen

NILAUS BILLE NIELSEN is one of the most promising and innovative young confectioners in Denmark. In 2007 he was awarded Young Chef of the Year and he also won Cake of the Year in 2003.

In 2001 he graduated as a confectioner from Kransekagehuset in Copenhagen, which was then run by confectioner Jørgen Søgaard Jensen. Nilaus Bille Nielsen was taught how to master the craft and acquired extensive knowledge about the art of confectionery, the characteristics of each ingredient and how they interact together in every recipe.

Following his apprenticeship he went to London in 2005 and was offered a position as pastry chef at a high-class restaurant. Here he gained a new perspective and knowledge about the sweet kitchen. 'It was a fantastic year where I got the chance to learn techniques as well as creating and developing a variety of cakes and desserts according to my own taste', he says. Nilaus Bille Nielsen has since assisted the restaurant in developing new dessert menus each season.

After returning to Denmark he was employed by Summerbird/Kransekagehuset and he is currently creating and developing cakes, desserts and chocolates for the company.

Nilaus Bille Nielsen enjoys the classical kitchen but his bent towards a more modern and approachable style in both taste and expression is evident in the following recipes. 'I like to share my sweet knowledge and create new recipes as well as finding new fun combinations, while always maintaining the characteristics of the ingredients', he says.

notes on marzipan ring cakes (Kransekage)

The marzipan ring cake dates back to medieval times and is known throughout Scandinavia. It is enjoyed at new-year celebrations, weddings, confirmations and other special events and festive occasions – often decorated with flags and figures. This traditional cake is comprised of rings that become progressively smaller. They are layered on top of each other in order to form a pyramid. In the following recipe, Nilaus has created marzipan cakes in squares, which is also common.

Another cake made with almonds is the Cornucopia, or Horn of Plenty, which is the hallmark of Danish confectioners and also served at special occasions. The sweeping horn is symbolic of food and abundance. According to the myth, the Cornucopia stems from Crete where the god Zeus survived on goat's milk for a few days. He then transformed a goat's horn into a symbol of fertility. The Cornucopia is filled with chocolates and biscuits.

Marzipan ring cakes (Kransekage)

400 g (14 oz) marzipan made with 70 percent almonds

120 g (4¼ oz) sugar

100 g (4 oz) egg whites

100 g (4 oz) almonds

Icing
100 g (4 oz) powdered sugar or icing sugar

approximately 1 tbsp boiling water

Utensils: knife, bowl, whisk, spoon, baking tray, baking paper, piping bag

Finely chop the almonds and whip them with sugar and egg whites until smooth. Set aside in a cool place until the sugar crystals are dissolved. Then gradually blend the egg mixture into the marzipan.

Form the mixture into tiny rectangular pieces weighing approximately 45 g (1½ oz). Place them on a baking tray lined with baking paper.

Bake the cakes in a preheated oven at 180 °C (350 °F) until they are lightly golden.

Decoration
The ring cakes are decorated by creating a zigzag pattern of icing using a piping bag. Many different types of decoration are possible, including nougat, preserved ginger, egg whites and icing sugar. The ring cake is decorated according to the occasion, for example with crackers or flags. For weddings the cake is crowned with a miniature bride and groom.

Icing
Blend icing sugar, cocoa powder and water.

marzipan

When purchasing marzipan, look for a minimum almond content of 60 percent and a golden shiny colour. The more almonds the marzipan contains, the better its quality will be.

Marzipan has been used in Europe for centuries and originated some time before the 10th century. From 1300 onwards many recipes that incorporated marzipan and imitation marzipan were developed in catholic Europe. In Denmark it was a luxury product used among the wealthy and royals.

Cold buttermilk soup
(Koldskål)

1 l (2 pt) cold buttermilk

Juice of 1½ lemons

40 g (1½ oz) egg yolk – approximately 2 eggs

90 g (3 oz) sugar

1 vanilla pod

Kammerjunkere

250 g (8 oz) flour

3 tsp baking powder

10 tbsp sugar

90 g (2.8 oz) butter

50 ml (1⅔ fl oz) full-cream milk

½ vanilla pod

1 egg

Utensils: whisk, bowl

Whip egg yolks and sugar with the seeds from the vanilla pod until light and fluffy. Then combine this mixture with the cold buttermilk and add lemon juice to taste. Serve while cold.

This dish is often enjoyed with *kammerjunkere*, which is described below. It can also be served with whipped cream or fresh berries.

Kammerjunkere
Utensils: bowl, blender or a whisk, rolling pin, baking tray, baking paper

In a bowl blend flour, sugar and baking powder together with the seeds from the vanilla. Soften the butter and add it to the flour mixture, kneading it into dough with milk and egg.

Place the dough in the fridge for about an hour to settle. On a floured bench or table roll it out to a 5-millimetre thickness. Cut circles approximately 3 centimetres in diameter. Place them on a baking tray lined with baking paper and bake in a preheated oven at 220 °C (430 °F) for about 8 minutes. Lower the oven temperature to 100 °C (210 °F) for approximately 20–30 minutes until the *kammerjunkere* dry out and become crisp. It is very important to turn the cakes upside down as well, so that they become thoroughly dry.

Koldskål is a traditional Danish recipe developed at the beginning of the 20th century. It is enjoyed mostly on warm summer days as either a snack or a dessert and is very popular throughout Denmark. In the 18th century koldskål was served as a first course and made of fruit juice, wine or beer spiced with lemon peel and nutmeg.

Nilaus Bille Nielsen has provided a traditional recipe, but adjusted the buttermilk and kammerjunkere recipes to a more contemporary style.

Chocolate and raspberry truffles

500 g (16 oz/1 lb) dark chocolate

250 g (8 oz) fresh cream

100 g (4 oz) raspberries

½ vanilla pod

Coating

500 g (16 oz/1 lb) chocolate, melted

400 g (14 oz) cocoa

Utensils: knife, 2 saucepans, sieve, spoon, confectionery thermometer, piping bag, baking tray, baking paper

Finely chop the chocolate, place it in a saucepan and melt it over low heat. In a separate saucepan, bring cream, raspberries and vanilla to a simmer. Pour the warm chocolate through a sieve, so that the chocolate becomes smooth, stirring it gently with small movements until it becomes homogenous.

Set aside the mixture until its temperature reaches 28 °C (82 °F). Fill a piping bag with the chocolate truffle and pipe small balls onto a baking tray lined with baking paper. Place the truffle balls in a cool place until the truffle has settled.

Coating
To coat, turn the truffles in the melted chocolate and roll carefully in the cocoa.

Red fruit porridge (Rødgrød) with elderflower mousse

250 ml (8 fl oz) milk

250 ml (8 fl oz) cream

100 g (4 oz) egg yolks

25 g (1 oz) sugar

30 g (1 oz) to 250 g (8 oz) dark chocolate

½ vanilla pod

Toasted cocoa beans, crushed

Red fruit porridge

200 g (7 oz) raspberries

100 g (4 oz) water

100 g (4 oz) cane sugar

2 tsp cornflour

100 g (4 oz) fresh strawberries and raspberries

½ vanilla pod

Elderflower mousse

180 g (6 oz) elderflower juice

½ vanilla pod

320 g (11 oz) cream

100 g (4 oz) sugar

120 g (4¼ oz) egg yolks

4 gelatine leaves

Mousse for the red fruit porridge

Utensils: spoon, saucepan, knife, confectionery thermometer, strainer, bowl, glass serving plates

In a bowl mix the egg yolks and sugar, blending them quickly, but not whipping them. Remove the vanilla seeds from the pod. In a saucepan, bring milk, cream and vanilla seeds to the boil. Finely chop the chocolate and put it aside. Pour a little of the warm milk over the egg yolk mixture and stir to combine. Pour the egg mixture into the remaining warm milk, which should thicken as the temperature is brought up to 75 °C (170 °C). Take off the heat and strain.

Pour the warm cream over the chopped chocolate to create an emulsion. Blend the toasted and crushed cocoa beans into the emulsion. Pour the mousse into glass serving dishes and refrigerate for two hours.

Red fruit porridge

Utensils: saucepan, muslin or sieve, tray

Bring 200 g (7 oz) raspberries and water to a gentle boil until the berries burst. Strain the liquid through a cloth (muslin for example) or a fine sieve. Split the vanilla pod, remove the seeds and add them to the raspberry juice with the sugar. Bring to a gentle boil and thicken with the cornflour. Allow to cool, then blend in the fresh berries. Pour the warm porridge on top of the chocolate mousse and store in a cool place before serving.

Elderflower mousse

Utensils: whisk, 2 bowls (one must be deep), knife, saucepan, confectionery thermometer, strainer, spoon

Blend the egg yolks carefully with the sugar. Place the gelatine in cold water for approximately 5 minutes, then squeeze well to remove water. Split the vanilla pod and remove the seeds, then add the elderflower juice and 200 g (7 oz) of the cream and boil gently. Pour a little bit of the warm cream over the egg yolks and stir well.

Add the gelatine, then pour the egg mixture back into the cream, which should thicken as the temperature is brought up to 75 °C (170 °F). Take off the heat and strain. Whip the remaining cream until light and fluffy. When the elderflower mixture's temperature lowers to 35 °C (95 °F) blend it with the lightly whipped cream. Pour the mousse into a deep bowl and put it in the fridge for about three to four hours or until it is has settled. Serve the red fruit porridge in portions on plates. Use a spoon heated in warm water to shape the mousse and place the elderflower mousse on top of the porridge.

The cake of the year 2003 with beer

250 g (8 oz) marzipan

100 g (4 oz) butter

150 g (5 oz) sugar

2 eggs

Lemon bavaroise

200 g (7 oz) full-cream milk

200 g (7 oz) of double cream

66 g (2 oz) egg yolks

16 g (½ oz) sugar

230 g (8 oz) milk chocolate

3 gelatine leaves

Finely grated peel and juice of 1 lemon

Preserved lemon

1 lemon, zested

20 g (¾ oz) sugar

20 ml (⅔ fl oz) water

Chocolate mousse

170 g (6 oz) vanilla cream*

200 g (7 oz) beer (preferably beer with a chocolate flavour, for example Carlsberg's Criollo stout)

230 g (8 oz) dark chocolate (for example 60 percent Valrhona)

1½ gelatine leaves

200 ml (7 fl oz) double cream

Dark chocolate chips (for decoration)

Mazarin
Utensils: bowl, spoon, mixer, baking tray, baking paper

Knead the marzipan, butter and sugar together. Add the eggs one at a time. Take care that the mixture does not become too light and airy, as it might collapse while baking.

In a mixer, blend the marzipan, butter, sugar and eggs together, then pour onto a baking tray lined with baking paper. The layer should be 1-centimetre thick. Bake in a preheated oven at 180 °C (350 °F) for 20 minutes. Cool and cut into suitably sized pieces.

Lemon bavaroise
Utensils: saucepan, spoon, confectionery thermometer, knife, cake rings

Bring milk and double cream to the boil, thicken with egg yolks and sugar while bringing to a temperature of 80 °C (175 °F). Soak the gelatine in cold water until it softens, then squeeze the excess water, and melt into the cream.

Chop the chocolate and pour over the warm cream.

Pour the cream into 10 cake rings approximately 4.5 centimetres in height and let them cool until settled.

Place the bavariose on top of the marzipan layers.

Preserved lemon
Utensils: knife, saucepan, bowl

Cut the lemon into thin slices.

Bring sugar and water to the boil and place the lemon slices in it, bring it to the boil for 2 minutes and refrigerate.

Chop the lemon finely and spread them over the lemon bavaroise.

Chocolate mousse
Utensils: saucepans, spoon

In a saucepan, warm the vanilla cream and melt the chocolate. In another saucepan, warm the beer and melt the gelatine directly in the beer until dissolved. Blend the cream and beer together. Allow to cool.

Whip the cream lightly and fold it into the cool chocolate cream. Spread the cream on top of the bavaroise.

To serve
Cut the mazarin into suitable sizes, place the bavaroise on top of the mazarin pieces, place the preserved lemon on top of the lemon bavaroise and then top with chocolate mousse.

Let the cake settle before decorating with dark chocolate chips just before serving.

*vanilla cream can bought in sachets from most supermarkets

This cake made by Nilaus Bille Nielsen was chosen as the 'Best Cake of the Year' by the Danish Bakery and Confectionery Organisation in 2003. The cake has a light lemon chocolate taste and a hint of beer.

Saison

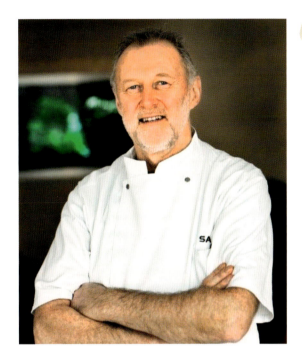

" Food should taste of what it is composed of. The basis of successful cooking is to consider the best of each piece of raw material and to bring out its own taste. Nordic cuisine is great. We pickle, preserve and smoke food "

Erwin Lauterbach

ERWIN LAUTERBACH HAS MADE a significant impact on Danish gastronomy. He has contributed to the development and the definition of New Nordic Cuisine and pioneered the use of local produce.

Erwin Lauterbach was born in Haderslev in Southern Jutland and became a chef in 1971. He began his career in Paris at Restaurant Copenhague where he met another brilliant Danish chef and developed a taste for cooking. During the two-and-a-half years he spent in Paris he worked with chefs from a 3-Michelin-star restaurant who were an enormous inspiration. He says, 'The French discipline and organisation in the kitchen, as well as respect for the Danish kitchen, is what Saison is based upon'.

Since 1981 Lauterbach has owned and managed Saison in Hellerup just north of Copenhagen, producing traditional and innovative food based on Danish and French recipes. Previously, Lauterbach established a restaurant in Malmø in Sweden called Primeur, which was awarded Best Restaurant of the Year, where he also made use of the best seasonal produce to create food of the highest quality.

Every day at 10 am Lauterbach gathers his team to get an overview of the daily deliveries. At this point, they assess the fresh fish and the new vegetables and mushrooms that will inspire the day's menu. Vegetables of the season play a central role at Lauterbach.

In 2001 Erwin Lauterbach received a Danish Gastronomy award in the Slow Food Competition for being at the top of his craft for 25 years. He was recognised for his honest kitchen, his sensuous and healthy food where vegetables star and for creating a friendly and positive atmosphere. In 2006 he also received the Danish Chef Award by the Foundation of the Advancement of Danish Gastronomy.

Pears in boiled elderberries, yoghurt ice cream and nuts in vanilla

6 pears

2 bunches of elderberries (you can also use blueberries or blackcurrants)

500 ml (16 fl oz/1 pt) water

100 g (4 oz) sugar

Yoghurt ice cream

650 g (23 oz) yoghurt

350 g (12 oz) crème fraîche

1.3 l (44 fl oz/2¾ pt) water

450 g (16 oz) sugar

Peel of 2 lemons

Vanilla boiled nuts

50 g (2 oz) whole almonds

50 g (2 oz) whole hazelnuts

50 g (2 oz) whole pistachios

500 ml (16 fl oz/1 pt) water

50 g (2 oz) sugar

1 vanilla pod

Serves 6

Utensils: peeling knife, saucepan, serving tray

Peel the pears and combine with elderberries, water and sugar. Boil, covered, until tender. Remove the pears and continue to boil the brine to a syrup-like consistency. Place the pears back in the condensed brine before serving.

Yoghurt ice cream
(makes enough for 15 people)

Utensils: ice cream machine or otherwise use a form.

Blend all the ingredients in an ice cream machine. Freeze.

Vanilla boiled nuts
(makes plenty)

Utensils: bowl, spoon, baking tray, baking paper, airtight container

Combine the nuts, almonds, pistachios, water and sugar with the seeds from the vanilla pod. Place on a baking tray lined with baking paper in a preheated oven at 125 °C (255 °F) until any liquid has evaporated. Shake the nuts to loosen any that are stuck together. Keep in an airtight container to maximise their shelf life.

To assemble
Place the pears on a plate with a little brine, sprinkle with the vanilla boiled nuts and add a ball of the yoghurt ice cream.

elderberries

Elder or elderberry is a shrub that grows up to 8 metres high. It is very common in Denmark and easy to handle as well as being frost resistant during spring. Elderberries are full of taste and as such are used in delicious soups or desserts, while elder flowers are sometimes used to flavour juice and tea. Elderberries are full of vitamins A, B and C.

berries

Berries are not only wonderful in desserts, they are also highly nutritious. Red berries are full of vitamin C, while blueberries are cleansing and good for balance, eye health and circulation.

Blueberries are blue or almost black with a violet-coloured juice. They do not ripen after harvest, so ensure they are ripe and firm when purchased. They are delicious in desserts, fruit salads or marmalade.

Soufflé pancakes with blueberries

20 g (¾ oz) melted butter

70 g (3 oz) flour

2 egg yolks

60 g (2 oz) sugar

Approximately 120 ml (4 fl oz) milk

2 egg whites

Approximately 200 g (7 oz) of blueberries

Icing sugar

Butter for the pan

(Makes 12–16 small pancakes)

Note: The batter can be made a couple of hours ahead.

Utensils: whisk, bowls, spoon, pan, strainer, baking tray, baking paper

Whisk the melted butter, flour, egg yolks, half of the sugar and the milk to make a batter. Whisk the egg whites with the remaining sugar until stiff, then fold it into the batter. Use a spoon to drop the batter onto a pan warmed with butter. Cook the pancakes on one side only and transfer them to a baking tray lined with baking paper. Keep the uncooked part of the pancake facing upwards.

Spread some of the blueberries on the pancakes.

Just before serving, sprinkle a fine layer of icing sugar over the pancakes and place under a warm grill or in the oven until the soufflés have browned.

Serve the pancakes while still warm with ice cream or berries folded through Greek yoghurt. Sweeten with a little icing sugar or Chantilly cream (cream whipped with sugar and sometimes vanilla seeds).

The blueberries can be replaced with gooseberries or halved plums, lightly baked with sugar. Raspberries, redcurrants, sea buckthorn or strawberries can also be used.

Meyers

> *"The true goal is global diversity – coherent local food cultures with strong identities"*
>
> Claus Meyer

CLAUS MEYER IS ONE OF Denmark's most well-known chefs. He has made a significant impact on Danish gastronomy and is a major player in the development and promotion of Nordic cuisine. His use and advocacy of seasonal produce is an inspiration to chefs throughout the Nordic countries.

Claus Meyer hosted a Danish TV series called *Meyer's Kitchen* and in 2006 took part in the international TV production *New Scandinavian Cooking*, where he tirelessly worked to promote new Nordic cuisine and thus pioneered the use of fresh produce in Scandinavia. He has published a number of cookbooks and has been a spokesperson and participant in public debate for almost 25 years, constantly raising awareness about improving food quality.

About 10 years ago Claus Meyer established Meyers Madhus (Meyer's Food House) with the aim of creating a place where food enthusiasts could meet chefs and experience the joy of preparing a great meal while they share the knowledge behind it. It has since become the nucleus of a unique gastronomic environment and has been visited by more than 40,000 people.

Throughout the years Claus Meyer has established a number of companies in Denmark, which together employ more than 350 people. In 2003 he founded Copenhagen gourmet restaurant Noma in collaboration with partner and executive chef René Redzepi. The restaurant has received two stars from the prestigious *Michelin Guide*. In 2010 the English magazine *Restaurant* named Noma the best restaurant in the world. Every year the magazine honours the 50 best restaurants in the world and the panel is made up of 806 food critics, chefs and gastronomes from 26 regions.

In 2006 Claus Meyer became an external lecturer at the Department of Food Science at the University of Copenhagen. In 2006 he was appointed adjunct professor within the research areas of food science. In 2009 he was assigned to a leading role in OPUS, a €15 million research project aimed at developing the 21st century's answer to the Mediterranean diet, 'The New Nordic Diet', and to investigate its potential health benefits.

Rhubarb trifle

500 g (16 oz) rhubarb
150 g (5 oz) sugar
½ vanilla pod
Peel and juice of ½ lemon

Fresh cheese cream
3 egg yolks (organic or pasteurised)
100 g (4 oz) cream cheese
100 ml (4 fl oz) double cream
50 g (2 oz) icing sugar
½ vanilla pod
Juice from rhubarb compote

Buckwheat macaroons
220 g (8 oz) hazelnuts
450 g (16 oz) icing sugar
215 g (7 oz) egg whites
50 g (2 oz) sugar
50 g (2 oz) buckwheat flour
brandy, vodka or another spirit (optional)

Rhubarb compote
Utensils: peeling knife, knife, bowl, ovenproof dish

Trim the tops and bottoms of the rhubarb stems. Rinse and cut into 2–3 centimetre pieces. Toss the rhubarb with sugar, seeds from the vanilla pod, grated lemon peel and lemon juice. Pour into an ovenproof dish and bake in a preheated oven at 150 °C (300 °F) for 20–30 minutes. Allow to cool before adding to the trifle.

Reserve the juice from the cooked rhubarb for use in the fresh cheese cream recipe.

Fresh cheese cream
Utensils: whisk, bowl

Mix the cream cheese with double cream, seeds from the vanilla pod and rhubarb juice. Whisk the egg yolks with icing sugar until it is white with a creamy texture. Blend the cream cheese and the egg mixture until it becomes a homogeneous trifle cream.

Buckwheat macaroons
Makes 60–70 macaroons

Claus Meyer loves these buckwheat macaroons, but if time is limited, you can use macaroons bought from a baker. Use curd cheese or drained junket if you are not able to access fresh cheese.

Utensils: food processor, strainer, bowl, whisk, piping bag, baking tray, baking paper

Preheat the oven to 145 °C (290 °F). Use a food processor to chop the hazelnuts until flour-like. Sift the hazelnut meal, icing sugar and buckwheat flour into a bowl.

Whisk the egg whites with sugar until firm. Working quickly, fold the dry ingredients into the egg whites. Put the mixture into a piping bag and pipe the macaroons (approximately 2 centimetres in diameter) onto a baking tray lined with baking paper. Let the macaroons sit for approximately 15 minutes before placing the tray in the middle of the oven. Bake for 12–15 minutes.

Before serving
Arrange the trifle in a transparent glass bowl or in individual glasses. Start with some of the macaroons, then drizzle with rhubarb juice and, according to taste, a small amount of vodka, brandy or other spirit. Add the cream and then the rhubarb. Repeat the process until the bowl or glass is filled up to the edge.

buckwheat flour

Buckwheat flour is made from the seeds of the crop plant buckwheat. It was introduced into Europe from Asia in the 14th century. Despite its name, it is not a cereal and is therefore suitable for people with gluten allergies.

rhubarb

Rhubarb was brought to Europe in the 1830s by an Italian botanist as a replacement for Chinese rhubarb, which was used in medicine. In Denmark rhubarb is primarily used to make red porridge or compote. The plant thrives in cold climates like Denmark's. Fresh rhubarb should be thin, springy and dark red in colour. Keep it in a cool place to maintain the moisture. Frozen rhubarb can be kept for a year. It is a delicious addition to soups, cakes and desserts, compotes, porridge and marmalade.

Bread 'n' butter pudding with rhubarb mash

300 g (10 oz) cleaned rhubarb cut into larger pieces

50–100 g (2 oz–4 oz) cane sugar, depending on the sweetness of the rhubarb

A little butter

Pudding
2 whole eggs

3 egg yolks

250 ml (8 fl oz) full-cream milk

250 ml (8 fl oz) cream

100 g (4 oz) cane sugar

Grains from 1 vanilla pod

1 pinch (⅛ tsp) sea salt

Approximately 300 g (10 oz) toasted bread, crust removed

150 g (5 oz) soft or melted butter

Cane sugar to sprinkle on top

Serves 10

Rhubarb mash
Utensils: pan, spatula

Sauté the rhubarb with butter and sugar, and possibly add a little water if necessary, for 5–10 minutes until it becomes a dense mash. Allow to cool slightly.

Pudding, filling and bread
Utensils: bowl, whisk, pastry brush, spring form or ovenproof dish

In a big bowl, blend the two whole eggs, three egg yolks, milk and cream with the sugar, salt and the vanilla pods. Mix thoroughly until all the sugar is dissolved. If possible let the mixture rest for half an hour.

Glaze the bread on both sides with the soft or melted butter. Also glaze the spring form or a small ovenproof buttered dish.

Cover the baking tray with half the bread, spread the rhubarb mash on top of the bread and then pour over half the egg mixture. Cover with the remaining bread and top with the remaining egg mixture.

Let the bread absorb the liquid for at least 15 minutes, sprinkle a little cane sugar on top and put the pudding into the oven at 180 °C (350 °F) for 45 minutes, or until the top of the bread is crisp and dark golden.

Allow to cool for half an hour before cutting and serving. If the pudding has been prepared the day before, warm it before serving.

A baked vanilla crème between crispy, caramelised bread served with fresh fruit compote or ice cream, this dish is a cross between crème brûlée and arme riddere (poor knights). If no suitable fruit is in season, you can leave out the compote and serve it with vanilla ice cream instead.

acacia honey

Acacia honey is commonly known as black locust, which is a tree native to North America and widely planted in Europe. In the US Acacia honey is also named 'American Acacia'.

Acacia honey is one of the most popular honeys because it stays in liquid form for a long time due to the high concentration of fructose. It has a hint of vanilla and flora and is recommended for sweetening purposes because of its lightness and lower acid content compared with other honeys.

Apple cake with syrup and cider

1.5 kg (3 lb) apples
100 ml (4 fl oz) unsweetened apple juice
50 ml (1⅔ fl oz) cider
½ vanilla pod
1 tbsp of Acacia honey

Cake
375 g (13 oz) hazelnuts
375 g (13 oz) sugar
225 g (8 oz) butter
2 whole eggs
2 egg whites
75 g (3 oz) flour

Serves 6

Cake filling
Utensils: peeling knife, knife, bowl

Core, peel and cut the apples into small pieces. Toss the apple pieces with the unsweetened apple juice, cider, seeds from the vanilla pod and honey. Infuse the apple pieces for 10–15 minutes.

Cake
Utensils: knife, whisk or blender, spring form pan

Finely chop the hazelnuts and mix with butter and sugar until soft and creamy. Add the two eggs, two egg whites and finally the flour. Pour the mixture into a greased 26-centimetre springform pan. Drain the apples, keeping the apple syrup. Spread the apples on top of the cake batter.

Bake the cake in the oven at 180 °C (350 °F) for 50–60 minutes. If the cake becomes too dark on top, cover it with foil until it has finished baking. Allow to cool.

Boil the apple syrup until thickened; then pour it over the cake. Serve with lightly whipped cream.

Note: This cake is ideally made the day before it is served as it can seem unfinished and soft in the middle immediately after it has been taken out of the oven. Be sure to cool the cake and let the apples rest as the pectin from the apples causes the cake to become firm.

Claus Meyer is famous for this apple cake, which is filled with apples, syrup and hazelnuts.

cider

Cider in Denmark was traditionally imported from Normandy, Bretagne, Germany, Switzerland and parts of the UK. Recently, however, cider production has become increasingly popular in Denmark. The climate is perfect for growing apples as it is quite similar to that of the French cider region.

Cider is made from fermented apple juice, which contains enough sugar to produce 5–6 percent alcohol. Like champagne, cider can be sweet or dry and contains some carbon dioxide from the fermentation process.

Many of Denmark's cider makers produce French-inspired farm cider using classical apple varieties from the island of Fejø, south of Zealand. Some use ordinary apples from Denmark. Different varieties of apple contain different acids and are categorised as sweet, sour, bitter-sour or bitter. All ciders contain these characteristics whether they are Danish, French or English. Danish apples contain plenty of acid and some are very sweet, which is why they are suitable for cider production. Cider made from bitter apples maintains its crispiness, structure and acidity. Sweet apples produce milder tasting cider with higher alcohol content. In 2005 six Danish fruit growers established Økologiske Cideræble Avlere (ØCA) (Organic Cider-apple Growers).

Apple soup with crisp apple rings

1 l freshly squeezed apples

3 slices of ginger (5 mm)

2 tbsp honey

½ lemon, sliced

1 apple cut into cubes for the soup

2 sprigs of mint, finely chopped

Crisp apple rings
2 sweet apples

25 g (1 oz) sugar

100 ml (4 fl oz) water

Serves 6

Accompaniment suggestion: 200 ml (7 fl oz) lightly whipped cream for the cold apple soup

Utensils: casserole dish, spoon

Combine all ingredients except the mint in a casserole dish and bring it to the boil for a few seconds, then add the finely chopped mint. Serve the soup with the crisp apple rings (see below).

Crisp apple rings

Bring water and sugar to the boil and cool.

Cut the apples into thin slices (1 millimetre) and dip into the cool sugar brine. Place the apple slices on a baking tray lined with baking paper, and dry them in the oven at 100 °C (210 °F) for 1–1½ hours until they are crisp but haven't lost their colour.

apples

Denmark has one of the biggest selections of apples in the world, including 700 varieties, many of which were created by mutation. The apple is the most significant fruit in Denmark. Some of the most popular varieties are Belle de Boskop, Ingrid Marie, Cox Orange, Filippa, Graasten and Guldborg, which can be found in the many gardens around Denmark. The Danish climate provides ideal growing conditions: a cool spring with nourishing rain and long summer days that are not too hot. There is a marked difference in temperatures from day to night, which results in apples with great structure as well as aromatic intensity and acidity.

Drained junket with compote of mirabelle plums and toasted oats

2 l (4 pt) junket

Toasted oats
200 g (7 oz) organic oats

3 tbsp honey

15 g (½ oz) butter

10 grains of sea salt

Mirabelle plum compote
500 g (16 oz) mirabelle plums

200 g (7 oz) cane sugar

Serves 6

Place the junket in a clean tea towel in a clean colander to remove the water. Drain the junket for a couple of hours until it has a silky texture and is approximately 1.3–1.5 litres (2½–3 pints) in volume.

For a thicker texture (similar to cream cheese) drain the junket for 4 hours.

Enjoy the drained junket with compote of mirabelle plums and toasted oats (see below) for breakfast.

Toasted oats
Utensils: pan, wooden spoon, tray

Gradually toast the oats in a pan until they become golden and crisp. Add honey, butter and salt to the pan and mix well with a wooden spoon, so that the oats become caramelised. Place the toasted oats on a tray to cool.

Mirabelle plum compote
Utensils: casserole dish, colander, spoon

Wash the mirabelle plums well and place them in a shallow casserole dish with sugar and add enough water to cover them. Boil the mirabelle plums until pulp and pips can be seen.

When the compote has boiled thoroughly, strain it so that the cherry pips stay in the colander and a lovely rough compote comes through. If there is too much water in the compote, reduce it further while constantly stirring.

DANISH CHEFS AWARD

The Danish Chefs Award is one of the most prestigious awards in Danish gastronomy. The award is unique because chefs working in the trade vote on who wins the award, which is announced once a year. Several hundred chefs in Denmark make nominations and provide explanations as to why they have voted for a particular chef.

The three chefs who receive the highest number of votes are short-listed and then all chefs vote again for one of these three chefs. The winning chef will have done something extraordinary for Danish gastronomy and she or he receives a bronze statue by Danish sculptor Erik Heide. This honour is awarded at a yearly fundraising event organised by the Foundation for the Advancement of Danish Gastronomy.

The Foundation for the Advancement of Danish Gastronomy was established in 2002 as an initiative of the Danish company Danish Crown with the aim to advance Danish cuisine by providing financial support to Danish chefs to attend courses and studies abroad.

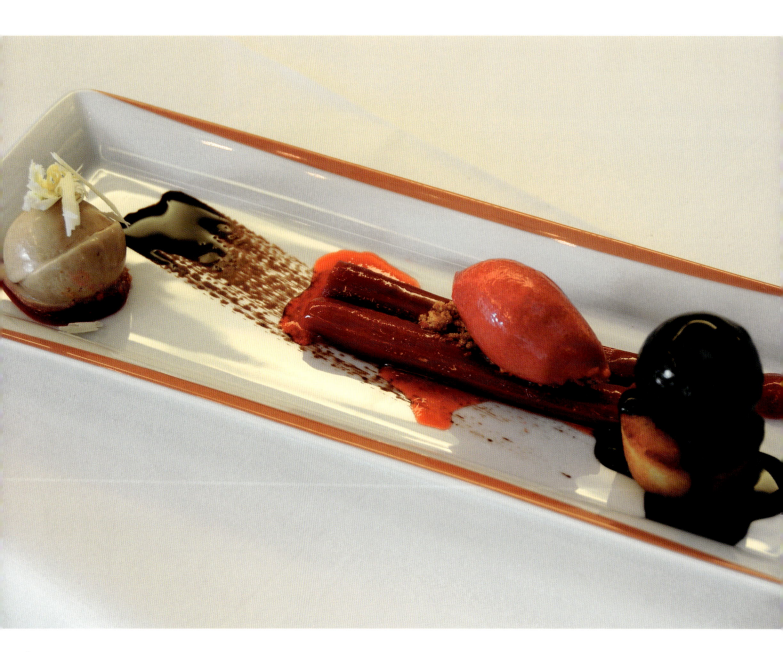

Le Sommelier

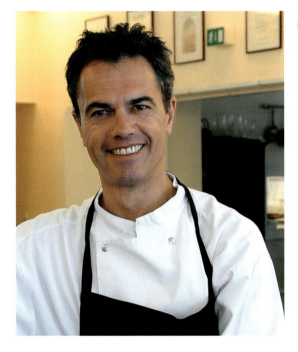

" *If a meal is to be optimal, you have to put your soul into it* "

Francis Cardenau

FRANCIS CARDENAU WAS BORN in Toulouse, France and became a chef in 1975. Since then he has worked with several highly acclaimed restaurants such as Taillevent and Le Copenhaque in Paris. In 1988 he moved to Denmark with his Danish wife and worked for Søllerød Kro (see page 66) and Kommandanten where he received two Michelin stars. Cardenau was the first chef in Denmark to gain two Michelin stars.

In 1997 Cardenau became kitchen chef and owner of Copenhagen restaurant Le Sommelier, where the French country kitchen is shown at its best in a cosy and informal atmosphere. He places an emphasis on using the best produce available that is still affordable for the majority of consumers and the restaurant has been a success ever since. Its wine selection – which features some of the world's best – is enormous.

'When I arrived in Denmark many years ago the most common ingredients in the Danish kitchen were carrots, cabbage, potatoes and fish,' Cardenau says, 'It was difficult to find any decent meat, but today the quality is very good.' Le Sommelier was the first restaurant in Denmark to serve the exclusive Wagyu beef from Japan. It is known worldwide for its naturally enhanced flavour and tenderness.

In 2007 Cardenau won the Danish Chefs Award, which was established to advance Danish gastronomy and to support Danish chefs with education abroad. The decision to honour Francis Cardenau as a master of taste and a mentor for a new generation of young talent was made by fellow chefs from around the country. Cardenau shows enthusiasm and commitment to the industry and has the ability and talent to make the most of the ingredients in his dishes.

In 2008 Francis Cardenau organised an event at Le Sommelier with Australian chef Tetsuya Wakuda and Spanish chef Sergi Arola with the aim of enhancing Danish gastronomy. It was organised in co-operation with the Foundation of the Chefs in Denmark trust, which received the profits from this event. It was a great success and will be repeated every year with various chefs around the world.

Francis Cardenau also owns the highly acclaimed French–Japanese restaurant Umami together with Sommelier Jesper Boelskifte and Erik Gemal, and in April 2009 they and Rasmus Oubæk opened Mash, a 'Modern American Steak House'. All three restaurants are situated in the heart of Copenhagen. Francis Cardenau is passionate about his profession and has a warm-hearted personality. 'I am always inspired to create something new and to inspire other chefs and young talent', he says.

Red fruit pudding with milk foam and almond ice cream

The Danish name for this red fruit pudding, rødgrød med fløde, is a tongue twister for foreigners and very much a part of Danish culture. Danes like to ask foreigners to say rødgrød, because it is almost unpronounceable for those not familiar with the Danish language. It is a popular dessert pudding in Denmark, especially during summer, possibly because its colour is reminiscent of the Danish flag. The traditional recipe uses redcurrants but it can be made with different types of red berries.

1 bunch of very red rhubarb

1 punnet of raspberries

1 punnet of blueberries

1 punnet of strawberries

4 tbsp sugar

500 ml (16 fl oz/1 pt) raw apples squeezed in a centrifuge (or unsweetened apple juice)

2 gelatine leaves

1 tbsp potato flour (or cornstarch/cornflour

Milk foam

200 ml (7 fl oz) organic milk

100 ml (4 fl oz) organic whipped cream

20 g (¾ oz) sugar

Seeds from 1 vanilla pod (preferably from pure Bourbon vanilla)

1 gelatine leaf

Almond ice cream

500 ml (16 fl oz/1 pt) organic full-cream milk

5 organic eggs or pasteurised eggs

50 g (2 oz) sugar

A little almond milk (orgeat syrup) without any artificial additives

Pudding

Note: for best results use organic products where possible

Utensils: paring knife/peeler, chopping knife, spoon, whisk, ovenproof dish, saucepan, bowl

Peel and cut rhubarb stems into small pieces. Wash all berries except for the raspberries. Split the strawberries and mix all berries except raspberries with sugar and apple juice. Place mixture in an ovenproof dish and bake in a preheated oven at 80 °C (175 °F) for an hour. Soak gelatine, then squeeze to remove excess water. Add raspberries and gelatine to the warm berries and allow to cool. If any juice is left, thicken it with potato flour if necessary.

Milk foam

Utensils: saucepan, bowl, spoon, whisk

Bring the milk to the boil with vanilla seeds and sugar. Soak the gelatine, then squeeze to remove excess water. Add the soaked gelatine and allow to cool; then add cream and whip it until it foams.

Almond ice cream

Utensils: saucepan, bowl, whisk, confectionery thermometer, ice cream machine, container for freezing

Bring milk to the boil. Whisk egg yolks with sugar until they become white and foamy. Pour milk over the egg blend and gently bring the mixture to 85 °C (185 °F) to thicken. Add almond milk until the mixture tastes of almonds. Allow the mixture to cool; then mix it in an ice cream machine until creamy. Freeze.

Serve the red porridge in soup bowls with a ball of ice cream and milk foam. For added texture sprinkle with toasted nuts spiced with a little cinnamon powder.

potato flour

Potato flour is starch derived from potatoes and made into flour. It is used in Scandinavia for baking and thickening sauces.

Vanilla cream with poached blueberries and tarragon, and blood orange and passionfruit sorbet

350 ml (12 oz) coffee creamer

4 pasteurised egg yolks

55 g (2 oz) cane sugar

Seeds from 1 vanilla pod

Poached blueberries

200 g (7 oz) wild blueberries

50 ml (1⅔ fl oz) water

50 g (2 oz) sugar

A little tarragon and Cointreau (orange liqueur)

Crumble

50 g (2 oz) flour

50 g (2 oz) icing sugar

50 g (2 oz) almond flour

50 g (2 oz) butter

Sorbet

300 ml (10 fl oz/½ pt) blood orange juice

200 ml (7 fl oz) passionfruit pulp

100 g (4 oz) sugar

Note: the poached blueberries can be made the day before to intensify the flavour.

Vanilla cream
Utensils: saucepan, bowl, whisk, baking tray or form

Warm the coffee cream with the vanilla seeds until almost boiling. Whisk the egg yolks and sugar until white. Blend the warm coffee cream with whisked eggs and sugar. Allow to cool. After an hour, pour the mixture into a deep baking tray or bowl and bake in the oven at 90 °C (195 °F) until it has settled. Allow to cool.

Poached blueberries
Utensils: saucepan, spoon

Bring water and sugar to the boil and boil for 3 minutes. Add the blueberries to the warm syrup, cool down and add Cointreau and tarragon to taste.

Crumble
Utensils: bowl, spatula, baking tray, baking paper

Use your fingers to blend ingredients together until the mixture is granulated. Spread the mixture on a baking tray lined with baking paper. Bake in a preheated oven at 160 °C (320 °F) until it becomes light brown. Allow to cool.

Blood orange and passionfruit sorbet
Utensils: saucepan, spoon, peeling knife, ice cream machine

In a saucepan warm the orange juice over low heat. Remove from heat when lukewarm. Melt the sugar in the lukewarm orange juice. Add the passionfruit pulp and use an ice cream machine to cool the mixture until it becomes creamy.

Place the blueberries on top of the vanilla cream with the crumble. Top with the sorbet and serve.

Warm chocolate ganache with mazarin, rhubarb and liquorice

100 g (4 oz) chocolate (70 percent cocoa)

130 g (5 oz) double cream

1 egg

Mazarin
50 g (2 oz) softened butter

50 g (2 oz) icing sugar

50 g (2 oz) marzipan

100 ml (4 fl oz) egg whites

Rhubarb sorbet
1 bunch (approximately 800 g) of very red rhubarb (allow 150 g/ 5 oz per person)

20 g (¾ oz) sugar per 100 g (4 oz)

20 g (¾ oz) water per 100 g (4 oz)

Liquorice parfait
50 g (2 oz) sugar

25 g (1 oz) water

50 g (2 oz) egg yolks

3 gelatine leaves

300 g (10 oz) of cream, lightly whipped

250 g (8 oz) white chocolate, melted

11 g (½ oz) liquorice powder

½ cup (4 fl oz) cream

Chocolate ganache
Utensils: saucepan, knife, whisk, spoon, springform pan

Bring the double cream to the boil and pour over the coarsely chopped chocolate. Add egg and mix well until it is very smooth.

Pour the chocolate cream into a small springform pan. Bake in preheated oven at 80 °C (175 °F) until it has settled. Allow to cool before removing from the springform pan.

Mazarin
Utensils: blender, spatula, springform pan

Mix together all ingredients and pour into a springform pan (the same size pan as used for the chocolate ganache) and bake in a preheated oven at 100 °C (195 °F) for approximately 25 minutes or until it has settled. Allow to cool.

Rhubarb sorbet
Utensils: paring knife/peeler, knife, ovenproof dish, saucepan, sieve, ice cream machine

Peel and cut the rhubarb into 15-centimetre lengths (2 pieces per person). Put aside approximately 500 grams of the rhubarb. Sprinkle a little sugar on the remaining rhubarb and place it in an ovenproof dish in a preheated oven at 100 °C (195 °F) until it becomes firm but not hard. Sprinkle with the rhubarb juice that is sometimes released during baking.

Weigh the rhubarb that was put aside. Add 20 grams (¾ ounce) of sugar and 20 grams (¾ ounce) of water per 100 grams (4 ounces) of rhubarb. Bring the rhubarb and sugar to the boil, then drain the liquid through a sieve. Allow the rhubarb to cool before mixing it in an ice cream machine.

Liquorice parfait
Utensils: saucepan, bowls, whisk, spoon, spatula, freezing forms

Bring sugar and water to the boil at 125 °C (255 °F). Allow to cool down a little. Whisk the egg yolks. Add the warm sugar and water to the egg yolks, a little at a time.

In a saucepan warm ½ cup (4 fluid ounces) full cream over heat. Remove from the heat and mix with the liquorice powder. Soak the gelatine in cold water, remove from the water and squeeze out the excess water. Dissolve the soaked gelatine in the warm creamy liquorice. Whisk the mixture until it has cooled. In a saucepan, melt the chocolate over moderate heat.

With a spoon, turn the sugar, water and egg mixture with whipped cream, chocolate and the liquorice mixture. Place the mixture in freezing forms and freeze. Sprinkle with cocoa powder before serving.

Serve the frozen rhubarb stems with liquorice parfait on top of the rhubarb sorbet. Place the chocolate ganache on top of the mazarin cake and place in a warm oven for a couple of minutes. Arrange the mazarin cake on a plate and decorate with melted chocolate.

TIVOLI GARDEN

Tivoli Garden is a famous amusement park in Copenhagen. It was opened in 1843 by founder and Danish entrepreneur Georg Carstensen, who told King Christian VIII, 'When people are amusing themselves, they do not think about politics'. The park is home to exotic buildings and beautiful illuminated gardens, amusement rides, top restaurants, concert halls and dinner shows. It is one of the oldest amusement parks in the world.

Restaurant Herman

> *Taste is to do with recollection. Everything we eat reminds us of something or someone. This is how our emotions work and how we stay connected to the world*
>
> Thomas Herman

EXECUTIVE CHEF THOMAS HERMAN PEDERSEN has a great passion for the classic Danish kitchen. He belongs to an elite group of Danish chefs who have been awarded numerous prizes and cooked in some of the world's best restaurants. In 2009 Thomas Herman and his staff received a star from the prestigious Michelin guide.

Restaurant Herman seats 40 and is situated in the heart of Tivoli, a large amusement park in Copenhagen. The restaurant is part of the Nimb building that includes an exclusive small hotel and a small delicatessen that promotes organic dairy products.

Thomas Herman was born in 1975 in Fredericia, Southern Jutland. He worked in many top restaurants in Jutland before working at Falsled Inn on Funen (see page 74). Herman also gained international experience by working for the three-Michelin-star restaurant Arzak in San Sebastian, and the two-Michelin-star restaurant La Broche in Spain. He later became an executive chef with the Michelin-starred Kong Hans Kælder in Denmark.

Thomas Herman remains true to his roots and the childhood memories that inspired him to create the recipes presented here. The bread layer cake originates from a traditional cake recipe of Southern Jutland. While still respecting traditional cooking he has made radical but loving changes to Danish desserts. He says, 'Food is filled with memories of smell and taste – it creates an atmosphere and conjures images while we eat. The best sauce I ever tasted was made by my grandmother – full of power and smell. I use both my memory and my gastronomic creativity while cooking.'

Bread layer cake (Brødtærte)

Made from rye bread, bread layer cake first appeared in recipe books in the 18th century and subsequently became very popular throughout Denmark.

The bread layer cake, with its alternating layers of whipped double cream and cake, was served at 'the big cake table' of Denmark (see p 82).

120 g (4 oz) egg yolks

180 g (6 oz) egg whites

100 g (4 oz) rye bread processed into breadcrumbs

250 g (8 oz) sugar

100 g (4 oz) finely chopped hazelnuts

1 tsp baking powder

200 g (7 oz) raspberry jam

Approximately 50 ml (1⅔ fl oz) double cream

Chocolate mix

500 g (16 oz/1 lb) dark chocolate, chopped

100 g (4 oz) cocoa butter

Utensils: whisk, bowl, blender, 3 baking trays, baking paper, spatula, spoon, knife

Preheat oven to 180 °C (350 °F). Whip the egg whites and sugar until a stiff meringue forms.

Mix the hazelnuts, rye breadcrumbs, and baking powder thoroughly; with a spoon fold the mixture gently into the meringue. Finish by folding in the egg yolks.

Spread thirds of the mixture evenly on three trays lined with baking paper and bake for approximately 10 minutes, or until the cake layers are golden brown. Allow to cool.

When cool, spread a very thin layer of raspberry jam on a cake layer and then add a layer of whipped cream. Top with another cake layer and repeat the process before ending with a thin layer of whipped cream. Freeze the cake for a couple of hours. Cut the cake into slices and freeze.

Chocolate mix for piping bag

Utensils: bowl, piping bag, spatula, plastic, knife

Place the chocolate and the cocoa butter into a bowl and melt above a water bath. Fill a piping bag with the mixture. Take the frozen cakes out of the freezer and spread the chocolate on top of the cakes in even layers.

To serve, warm 100 grams (4 ounces) of dark chocolate and spread it very thinly on a piece of plastic. Once set, cut the chocolate into small pieces and serve the cake slightly cool on top of the chocolate pieces.

Decorate the cake with drops of condensed milk.

> *The motivation is to spoil the guests, to see the the joy they get from indulging in a perfect meal. This happiness around the dinner table — I will do anything for it*
>
> Jakob de Neergaard

21st-century raspberry canapé (Hindbærsnitte)

250 g (8 oz) cream

250 g (8 oz) raspberries

80 g (3 oz) sugar

4 gelatine leaves

Raspberry marmalade
500 g (16 oz/1 lb) frozen raspberries

325 g (11 oz) sugar

8 g (½ oz) pectin

Peel of 1 lemon, thinly sliced

Tart
125 g (4 oz) cold butter

100 g (4 oz) icing sugar

250 g (8 oz) wheat flour

1 egg

Icing
200 g (7 oz) icing sugar

Approximately 20 g (¾ oz) pasteurised egg whites

Raspberry pannacotta
Utensils: blender, strainer, saucepan, bowl, spoon, spatula, oval or semicircle forms for freezing

Blend the raspberries, sugar and cream. Strain the mixture into a small saucepan over medium heat.

Put the gelatine in iced water and set aside. After 5 minutes, remove the gelatine from the water and squeeze out the excess water, then pour the gelatine into the warm blend of cream. Stir well. Pour the cream into small oval or semi-circle forms and place in the freezer.

Raspberry marmalade
Utensils: peeling knife, blender, spoon, bowl, saucepan

Blend 200 grams (7 ounces) of the sugar with the berries. Mix pectin with the rest of the sugar and combine it with the berries. Pour the mixture into a saucepan and simmer over low heat for approximately 45 minutes, ensuring that the mixture does not boil. Allow to cool before adding lemon peel.

Tart
Utensils: bowl, blender, rolling pin, knife, a cup or circle cutter, baking tray, baking paper

Knead all ingredients together until consistent and smooth and place in the fridge for a couple of hours. Roll out the dough as thinly as possible then place in the fridge for another hour. Cut the dough into small circles of desired size and place on a baking tray lined with baking paper. Bake in a preheated oven at 170 °C (340 °F) for approximately 6 minutes until golden brown.

Icing
Utensils: bowl, spoon, whisk, spatula

Pour the icing sugar into a bowl and slowly stir in the egg whites until the icing is stiff.

To serve: Spread a little marmalade between two pieces of the tart. Place a pannacotta on top, add a little drop of icing and decorate with lemon thyme.

The raspberry canapé dates back to the 18th century when it was called Vienna tart (Wienertærte) or Vienna cake (Wienerkage). At this time it consisted of many thin layers, some made with almond flour, different types of jam between the layers and colourful icing. By the beginning of the 21st century the cake had been pared back to just one layer with raspberry jam.

French nougat with a taste of dream cake

This 'taste of dream cake' originates from a cake of the same name that became fashionable during the 1960s. At that time, the roasting dish cake was in favour because it was easy to prepare in a busy household and it lasted a lot longer than a layer cake.

Saucepan 1
500 g (16 oz/1 lb) sugar
500 g (16 oz/1 lb) brown sugar
125 g (4 oz) glucose
100 g (4 oz) water

Saucepan 2
500 g (16 oz/1 lb) honey
75 g (3 oz) glucose

Food mixer
220 g (8 oz) egg whites
50 g (2 oz) sugar
400 g (14 oz) toasted coconut
100 g (4 oz) chopped pistachios

Utensils: saucepans, food mixer or blender, confectionery thermometer, baking paper, spoon, knife

In saucepan 1, bring sugar, brown sugar, glucose and water to the boil at 157 °C (314 °F). In a food mixer, whip the egg whites and the sugar until it forms a stiff meringue, pour over the warm glucose mixture and continue to whip at low speed until smooth.

In saucepan 2, bring honey and glucose to the boil at 122 °C (251 °F) and pour it into the meringue. Whip the meringue at high speed for approximately 40 minutes and then add coconuts and pistachios. Pour the mixture between two pieces of baking paper and roll to a thickness measuring 1 centimetre. Leave the mixture overnight in a cool place, then cut into desired size. Roll in finely chopped pistachios.

Red porridge flavoured marshmallow cream (Rødgrød med fløde som marshmallow)

200 g (7 oz) sugar
40 g (1 oz) glucose
90 g (4 oz) water
70 g (3 oz) egg whites
3½ gelatine leaves
16 drops of strawberry extract
6 drops of food colouring

Strawberry marshmallow
Note: make the marshmallow the day before

Utensils: bowl, saucepan, confectionery thermometer, whisk, piping bag

Place the gelatine in iced water. Boil the sugar, water and glucose to 145 °C (295 °F). When the temperature reaches 140 °C (280 °F) start to whip the egg whites until they become a meringue, then pour the syrup at 145 °C (295 °F) over the meringue and continue to whip. Remove the gelatine from the water, squeeze to remove excess water, and dissolve it in a saucepan over moderate heat. Add the meringue to the bowl over moderate heat, add the colour and the essence into the bowl, and whip for another 30 minutes. Using a piping bag, squeeze small drops and decorate with dried strawberries and raspberries. Keep overnight before serving.

Inspiration of biscuit cake
(Inspiration of kiksekage)

100 g (4 oz) cream

25 g (1 oz) sugar

30 g (1 oz) pasteurised egg yolks

75 g (3 oz) chocolate

Choko tuille
100 g (4 oz) glucose

100 g (4 oz) fondant sugar

45 g (1½ oz) dark chocolate (65% cocoa)

Chocolate creme for *kiksekage* (to be made the day before)
Utensils: saucepan, bowl, food mixer or blender, spoon, confectionery thermometer

In a saucepan, bring cream and sugar to the boil. Pour the mixture into a bowl, adding the egg yolks and whipping until mixture becomes homogeneous. Pour the cream mixture back into the saucepan and warm to 75 °C (165 °F) while stirring. Add the chocolate while the mixture is still warm and stir until smooth. Refrigerate overnight.

Choko tuille
Makes plenty, but it will keep for a long time

Serving suggestion: add small chocolate eggs to the cocoa flame and decorate with sea salt

Utensils: saucepan, knife, spoon, silicone mat, cling film, spatula, fork

In a heavy-based saucepan bring glucose and fondant sugar to the boil at 163 °C (325 °F). Chop the chocolate finely and then add the syrup, blending very carefully. Pour the mixture onto a silicone mat and allow it to cool. When the mixture is hard, break the chocolate into pieces and wrap individually with cling film (they will keep for a long time). Warm one of the pieces in a preheated oven at 100 °C (210 °F). When chocolate is soft, use a spatula and your thumb or a fork to draw 'flames'. This might take some practice, but you will soon get the hang of it.

When, as an adult, Thomas Herman tasted the biscuit cake he used to enjoy when he was a child, he found that the cake, which dates back to the beginning of 20th century, was a bit heavy and greasy for his adult palate. So he decided to make a new version without the oil and vegetable fat used in the original recipe.

rye bread

Danish rye bread, or rugbrød, is highly regarded among the Danes and is used in some of the recipes in this book. Rye bread is enjoyed in Denmark's famous open sandwiches, called 'smorgasbord', in porridge and in cakes and desserts. The base for this bread is sourdough made with rye flour and rye grains. It comes in many variants with different seeds.

Coffee bread from Fredericia
(Kaffebrød som i Fredericia)

Coffee bread originated in Jutland, although it also appeared in Zealand around the same time. One of the original recipes, and possibly the oldest, is from Luise Beate Augustine Friedel's 1795 book, New and Complete Confectionery Book, Copenhagen.

Coffee bread was then made of lemon, bitter orange peel and whipped egg whites. In the 1960s coffee bread developed into small toasted bread with macaroons.

100 g (4 oz) marzipan

60 g (2 oz) sugar

1 egg white

Coffee nougatine

225 g (8 oz) fondant powder

150 g (5 oz) glucose

20 g (¾ oz) butter

1 pinch of salt

25 g (1 oz) instant coffee

Brioche

Two slices of brioche, a couple of days old

Cocoa icing

100 g (4 oz) powdered sugar or icing sugar

approximately 1 tbsp cocoa

approximately 1 tbsp boiling water

Macaroons

Makes approximately 8 pieces

Utensils: blender, bowl, piping bag

In a bowl, mix the sugar with the egg white, then heat over a water bath for approximately 15 minutes (or until the sugar has dissolved).

Gradually blend the egg white mixture into the marzipan, and finish by whipping the mixture thoroughly. Fill a piping bag with the mixture in and place it in the refrigerator. You can easily make this recipe in larger quantities because it can be frozen.

Coffee nougatine

Utensils: saucepan, confectionery thermometer, blender, strainer, silicone mat, glass for marking out, baking tray, baking powder

Bring the glucose and fondant powder to boil at 160 °C (320 °F). Add butter and blend until homogeneous. Cool the caramel and blend it until it becomes a fine powder, then blend with the instant coffee. Strain the powder mixture onto a silicone mat and mark 3-centimetre circles in the powder.

Bake on a tray lined with baking paper in a preheated oven at 150 °C (300 °F) for approximately 3 minutes. Remove carefully from the baking tray.

Brioche and completion

Utensils: knife, bowl, baking tray, baking paper, spatula

Cut small 2.5-centimetre circles in the brioche slices and pipe the macaroon mixture onto the circles. Bake on a baking tray lined with baking paper in a preheated oven at 180 °C (350 °F) for approximately 7 minutes or until the macaroons are golden brown.

Before serving assemble the brioche with the coffee nougatine on top, then add a drop of icing on the nougatines.

Cocoa icing

Blend icing sugar, cocoa and water.

Veiled farm girl
(Bondepige med slør som smørrebrød)

Half a loaf of day-old ciabatta bread

A little olive oil

Approximately 200 g (7 oz) double cream

Seeds from ½ vanilla pod

Membrillo (Spanish quince paste)

Fresh chervil

50 g (2 oz) quince tea processed into fine powder and mixed to taste with 100 g (4 oz) icing sugar

Hint: To create a wonderful vanilla sugar keep the vanilla pod after the seeds have been extracted and place in a jar with sugar.

Cut the bread into the thinnest possible slices (it is easier if the bread is slightly frozen).

Brush the slices with a little olive oil and bake in the oven at 160 °C (320 °F) for approximately 5 minutes or until the bread is golden. Blend the membrillo until smooth (add a little lemon juice if necessary), strain and pour it into a piping bag. Whisk the cream with the vanilla seeds until stiff.

To serve add 4 drops of membrillo on top of the toasted ciabatta bread, a little cream (about the size of an egg) and four leaves of chervil. Finally scatter the tea powder over the top.

This recipe was created before ovens and stoves were widely available. It is still very popular today, and is very similar to apple cake; the difference being that apple cakes are made with macaroons rather than bread. The first known recipe for veiled farm girl was created by Christine Rostrup in 1848. The dessert's name comes from its down-to-earth ingredients and just like any practical farm girl, who does her job effectively and quickly, this dessert is quick to prepare.

Thomas Herman uses vanilla because it is distinctive, powerful and lightly spicy. He advises purchasing Polynesian vanilla (from Tahiti), but Bourbon vanilla is also suitable.

THE MICHELIN GUIDE

The Michelin Guide is the most famous and influential gastronomy rating in the world. The guide awards one to three stars to a small number of restaurants of outstanding quality. One star means 'a very good restaurant in its category', two stars mean 'excellent cooking and worth a detour' and 3 stars mean 'exceptional cuisine and worth the journey'. In Denmark The Michelin Guide only evaluates restaurants in the Copenhagen area.

Søllerød Kro (Søllerød Inn)

> *It is all about getting the simplicity to appear exquisite*
>
> Jakob de Neergaard

SØLLERØD INN IS SITUATED in one of the most picturesque regions of Denmark in Northern Zealand, just north of Copenhagen, where one can still find village ponds, old timber-frame houses and beautiful gardens. Situated next to an old castle and the local church, the inn was built during the summer of 1677 when the local priest was given license to establish and run an inn for the parish and visitors. The stable of this inn is now an à la carte restaurant and the large barn, with its old panels and collar beam still intact, is a function room seating 160.

For decades, Søllerød Inn has been one of the most prestigious and highly awarded restaurants in Denmark and some of the best chefs in Denmark have worked there. Since 2002 chefs Jakob de Neergaard and Jan Restorff have maintained Søllerød's position among the most renowned and respected eating places in Denmark. In 2007 Søllerød Inn received a prestigious star from *The Michelin Guide*. Jakob de Neergard has gained international experience with Alain Ducasse and at the Hotel Ritz in Paris as well as Michelin-star restaurants in Belgium, among others.

Two other young Danish chefs are also contributing to the high standard at Søllerød Inn today. Nicolas B George graduated with distinction from Munkebo Kro in 2005 and has gained numerous awards while working for Le Sommelier (see page 52) and Bøgen and Moi in Kristiansand in Norway. Daniel Kruse graduated as a chef in 2002 and as a confectioner in 2005 and has received numerous awards for his cuisine including 'Best young confectioner in Denmark' as well as winning the Nordic Championship in 2006. He previously worked at Restaurant Saison (see page 40).

Although the restaurant oozes elegance, the atmosphere is relaxed and unpretentious. The menu is based on French cuisine and Danish raw produce with a touch of innovation. Their signature dishes are oysters, foie gras and truffles and Danish vegetables from Lammefjorden in Northern Jutland. Also Søllerød Inn is a paradise for dessert lovers and Nicolas B George and Daniel Kruse have kindly provided the mouth-watering dessert recipes that follow.

In 2009 Søllerød Inn received the award for the best restaurant in Denmark and its wine list – which consists of 1700 wines, the majority of which are French, Italian and German – was awarded the best in the Nordic countries.

Rhubarb with strawberries and almonds

1 kg (2 lb) of very red rhubarb, chopped into squares

1 l (2 pt) water

1.25 kg (2 lb 8 oz) sugar

100 g (3 oz) glucose

2 gelatine leaves

Compote
300 g (1 oz) very red rhubarb

200 g (7 oz) strawberries

200 g (7 oz) sugar

Seeds from ½ vanilla pod

Juice of 1 lemon

Milk gel
1 l (2 pt) whole milk

300 g (10 oz) cream

200 g (7 oz) sugar

39 gelatine leaves

Cream mousse
500 g (16 oz/1 lb) cream, lightly whipped

100 g (4 oz) egg yolks

80 g (3 oz) sugar

2 gelatine leaves

1 vanilla pod

Milk gel

Marzipan pearls
300 g (10 oz) full-cream milk

200 g (7 oz) marzipan

9 gelatine leaves

1 l (2pt) cold olive oil

Rhubarb sorbet
Utensils: saucepan, spoon, blender, ice cream machine

Place gelatine in cold water for approximately 5 minutes until softened, then squeeze out the excess water. In a saucepan of warm water, sugar and glucose, add gelatine and stir until gelatine is dissolved. Remove from heat. Add chopped raw rhubarb and blend. Churn the mixture in an ice cream machine to create sorbet.

Strawberry and rhubarb compote
Utensils: bowl, spoon, hemispherical moulds, piping bag

Combine all ingredients and bring to the boil until the rhubarb and fruit is tender. Freeze half of the mixture, preferably in hemispherical moulds, and fill a piping bag with the other half. Add the small frozen hemispheres to the mousse in the recipe below.

Milk gel
Utensils: bowl, spoon, confectionery thermometer

Combine all ingredients and allow to set at 45 °C (110 °F).

Ball of cream mousse and rhubarb from hemisphere moulds
Utensils: whisk, bowl, spoon, hemispherical moulds, form for freezing, skewer

Whisk the eggs with sugar and vanilla until light and fluffy. Melt gelatine in water for approximately 5 minutes, remove the gelatine and squeeze out the excess water. Add the gelatine to the eggs and turn in the whipped cream.

Pipe the mixture into hemispherical shapes. In the centre, place a frozen hemisphere of strawberry/rhubarb compote. Smooth and freeze. When completely frozen take it out of the form and add hemispheres together, so that it creates a ball. One by one put each ball onto a skewer and dip it into the milk gel.

Marzipan pearls
Decoration: rhubarbs, strawberries and finely chopped toasted almonds

Utensils: saucepan, spoon, bowl, tea towel, 1-litre jug

In a saucepan, warm the milk with the marzipan and mix with a spoon. Soak gelatine in cold water for approximately 5 minutes, then remove and squeeze out any excess water.

Strain the marzipan mixture through a clean tea towel and pour it into a litre jug, add the gelatine and stir until dissolved. Drip mixture into cold olive oil to form pearls. Wash the pearls to remove oil.

Place the rhubarb sorbet on a plate and add the strawberry and rhubarb compote. Top with ball of cream mousse and rhubarbs; then add the milk gel and marzipan pearls. Surround with a ring of finely chopped rhubarb and strawberries with finely chopped toasted almonds.

strawberries

The most common varieties of strawberries in Denmark are Deutsch Evern, J.A. Dybdahl and Zefyr and Senga Sengana. Danish strawberries are very aromatic and have a powerful flavour. Strawberries have been cultivated since antiquity and were introduced to Denmark during the Renaissance. The berries are full of vitamin C and 150 grams covers the daily requirement for this vitamin. Strawberries also contain manganese, iron, calcium and folic acid.

Apples, hazelnuts and herbs

350 g (12 oz) full-cream milk

50 g (2 oz) double cream

120 g (4 oz) low-fat sour milk product or cultured product

150 g (5 oz) toasted hazelnuts

90 g (3 oz) sugar

70 g (2 oz) glucose

A pinch of salt

Apple consommé
Juice of 1 kg (2 lb) apples

Lemon or crushed vitamin C tablets (to prevent the juice becoming brown)

Apple purée
500 g (16 oz/1 lb) apples (peeled and cored)

Lemon juice or crushed vitamin C

20 g (¾ oz) sugar

Hazelnut malto
2 tbsp malto

1 tbsp hazelnut oil

Hazelnut tuile
100 g (4 oz) butter

200 g (7 oz) sugar

75 g (3 oz) flour

100 g (4 oz) white wine

Chopped hazelnut

Herbs
Lemon balm

Mint

Ground ivy

Hazelnut ice cream
Utensils: blender, confectionery thermometer, spoon, freezing tray or ice cream machine

In a blender, mix everything together at 37 °C (100 °F). Pour the mixture into a freezing tray and stir every half an hour until smooth. Alternatively, use an ice cream machine to achieve the same effect.

Apple consommé
Utensils: blender, bowl

Blend apple juice with lemon or vitamin C. Keep cool.

Apple purée
Utensils: saucepan, blender

Steam the apples with vitamin C (or lemon juice) and sugar until tender. Blend to a fine purée. Allow to cool.

Hazelnut malto
Utensils: whisk, bowl

Whip malto and hazelnut oil together until it becomes like 'snow'.

Hazelnut tuile
Utensils: whisk, bowl, buttered tray, spoon

Whip together butter, sugar, flour and wine. Place on a buttered tray and sprinkle with hazelnuts. Bake in preheated oven at 180 °C (350 °F) until golden. Make tuiles using an egg cup.

Place the hazelnut ice cream on a plate next to the apple consommé. Add apple purée on top of the apple consommé and decorate the hazelnut ice cream with herbs, hazelnut malto and tuile.

Raspberry, caramel and rosehips

250 g (8 oz) raspberry purée (see recipe opposite) or boiron

6.2 g (¼ oz) pectin

288 g (10 oz) sugar

55 g (2 oz) glucose

3.5 g (⅛ oz) citric acid

Dipping gel
300 g (10 oz) raspberry purée

100 g (4 oz) sugar

Juice of ½ lemon

10 gelatine leaves

Raspberry balls
200 g (7 oz) cream

100 g (4 oz) raspberry purée

Raspberry sorbet
1 kg (2 lb) raspberries

200 g (7 oz) sugar

250 g (8 oz) liquid glucose

100 g (4 oz) water

125 g (4 oz) glucose

3 gelatine leaves

White chocolate with cream
White chocolate half shell

100 g (4 oz) cream

Rosehips pearls
1 kg (2 lb) rosehip leaves

50 g (2 oz) sugar

50 ml (1⅔ fl oz) water

3 gelatine leaves

olive oil

Note: Start rosehip pearls the day before

Raspberry paté de fruit
Utensils: saucepan, serving trays, spoon

Bring raspberry purée to the boil with the pectin and 28 grams (approximately 1 oz) of sugar. Add 260 grams (approximately 9 oz) of sugar while bringing it to the boil at 109 °C (222 °F). Add glucose and citric acid. Arrange onto serving trays while warm.

Gel for dipping
Utensils: saucepan, spoon

Soak the gelatine in cold water until softened. Squeeze to remove excess water. Place all ingredients including the gelatine in a saucepan and heat to 43 °C (88 °F).

Stir until the gelatine is dissolved.

Raspberry balls
Blend cream and raspberry purée and fill hemisphere moulds with the mixture. Freeze. When frozen, remove from the moulds and place them onto a skewer to dip into raspberry gel.

Raspberry sorbet
Utensils: blender, bowl, strainer, saucepan, ice cream machine

Soak the gelatine in cold water for approximately 5 minutes, remove and squeeze to remove excess water. Mix together all ingredients until the gelatine has dissolved and everything is combined. Strain the mixture, then use an ice cream machine to freeze.

White chocolate with cream
Fill the chocolate with cream and finish off with white chocolate.

Rosehips pearls
Start the day before.

Utensils: blender, strainer, bowl, spoon

Combine rosehip leaves, sugar and water and set aside until the following day. Strain.

Soak the gelatine in water for approximately 5 minutes. Squeeze to remove excess water. Then add the gelatine to the strained liquid and stir until dissolved. Drip the liquid into cold olive oil to form small pearls. Rinse the pearls in cold water to remove oil.

Place the raspberry sorbet on a plate with raspberry paté de fruit, decorate using white chocolate with cream and top with rosehip pearls, raspberry balls and gel for dipping.

rosehips

Rosehips consist of soft fruit meat with seeds that must be removed. Rosehips have a high concentration of vitamins A and C as well as calcium. When raw they must be consumed within a couple of days.

Caramel glass tuile
100 g (4 oz) isomalt or sugar

100 g (4 oz) glucose

100 g (4 oz) fondant mass (optional)

20 g (¾ oz) cocoa

Raspberry purée
100 g (3 oz) raspberry purée

20 g (¾ oz) sugar

Seeds from ½ vanilla pod

Caramel glass tuile *(optional decoration)*
Utensils: saucepan, food-blender, spoon

Bring isomalt or sugar, glucose and fondant to the boil at 90 °C (184 °F). If using sugar, boil at 160 °C (320 °F). Add the cocoa. Allow to cool before starting the next step. Blend to a fine powder and bake at 110 °C (125 °F) until melted again (approximately 5 minutes).

Raspberry purée
Utensils: saucepan, spoon

Bring all ingredients to a gentle boil. Allow to cool before serving.

blackberries

Blackberries are juicy and aromatic blue-black stone fruits, and can be found in the majority of Danish woods. The berries have a high fibre content, as well as containing folic acid and vitamin C. They are delicious in fresh salads, cakes and preserves.

Passionfruit, cream chocolate and wood sorrel

200 g (7 oz) chocolate

Passionfruit meringues
100 g (4 oz) passionfruit pulp

100 ml (4 fl oz) egg whites

80 g (3 oz) sugar

20 g (¾ oz) cocoa

Crisp passionfruit pulp
250 g (8 oz) passionfruit pulp

3.5 g (¼ oz) pectin

Passionfruit parfait
200 g (7 oz) double cream

100 g (4 oz) passionfruit pulp

20 g (¾ oz) sugar

1 gelatine leaf

Fresh wood sorrel or mint

'Bridges' of cream chocolate
Utensils: saucepan, spatula, piece of plastic, knife

In a saucepan melt the chocolate over low heat. Spread a thin layer of the chocolate on a piece of plastic. Cut into small rectangles.

Passionfruit meringues
Utensils: saucepan, whisk, knife, spoon, dehydrator, piping bag

Bring the sugar and juice to the boil. Whip the sugar and juice mixture with egg whites until stiff. Use half of the mixture to create small circles with a spoon, and dry them in a dehydrator. Fill a piping bag with a small nozzle with the other half of the mixture.

Crisp passionfruit pulp
Utensils: bowl, spoon, spatula, baking paper or Teflon paper, dehydrator

Mix the ingredients and bring to the boil for a minute. Let the mixture rest for 10 minutes. Spread very thinly onto Teflon or baking paper. Dry for 24 hours in dehydrator.

Passionfruit parfait
Utensils: whisk, bowl, saucepan, spoon, piping bag

Lightly whip the cream. Soak gelatine in cold water for 5 minutes, remove from water and squeeze to remove excess water. In a saucepan warm the pulp at low heat, add sugar and gelatine, and stir until the gelatine has dissolved. Allow to cool before blending with cream. Use a piping bag to create pyramid shapes and freeze.

Use wood sorrel or mint as decoration.

Funen

Falsled Kro (Falsled Inn)

" When cooking use the best possible ingredients and put your heart into it "

Per Hallundbæk and Randi Schmidt

FALSLED INN IS SITUATED IN a beautiful area of Denmark in the southern part of the island Funen, which lies between Jutland and Zealand.

Per Hallundbæk, Director and Executive Chef, and his wife Randi Schmidt, Managing Director, have managed Falsled Inn since the beginning of 2009. Schmidt is originally from Southern Jutland and Hallundbæk is from Funen.

Prior to managing Falsled Inn Schmidt and Hallundbæk spent eight years at Hotel Engø Gård, which is situated on an island 100 kilometres south of Oslo in Norway. Initially, they had 10 employees, but by the end of their stay they had turned Hotel Engø Gård into an internationally regarded restaurant with 55 employees during the peak season. During this time Hallundbæk received several awards, including, among others, an award for outstanding achievement in staff development, while Schmidt received an award for 'Young leader of the year' in Norway. Hotel Engø Gård is mentioned in the prestigious guides Le Grandes Tables Du Monde and Relais & Chateaux. Falsled Kro is the only Danish restaurant to be mentioned in these guides.

Schmidt and Hallundbæk share a vision of creating and maintaining an inspiring and motivating environment at the Falsled Inn so that employees enjoy their working life and feel they are part of a team. Schmidt and Hallundbæk regularly visit other top restaurants for experience and inspiration. 'We are very humble about this beautiful place. It is an honour to be asked to manage Falsled Inn,' says Hallundbæk. Schmidt and Hallundbæk are successors to the highly acclaimed Jean-Louis Lieffroy, who retired at the end of 2008. Hallundbæk was previously employed as an executive chef with Fakkelgaarden in Southern Jutland (see page 84).

Falsled Inn was bought by the Grønlykke family in 1970. The family also own Restaurant Herman (see page 58). The menu at Falsled Kro is classic Danish–French and the restaurant is highly regarded for its fresh, high-quality meals served in elegant surroundings.

The following dishes created by Hallundbæk are based on fresh local produce from the island of Funen.

Sea buckthorn, carrots and crisp rye bread with liquorice

250 ml (8 fl oz) milk

250 ml (8 fl oz) cream

100 g (4 oz) sea buckthorn (or passionfruit)

125 g (4½ oz) sugar

5 egg yolks

1 tbsp of glucose

Carrot purée with sea buckthorn

300 g (10 oz) carrots, peeled and cut into small pieces

100 g (4 oz) sea buckthorn (or passionfruit)

5 tbsp honey

200 ml (7 fl oz) cream

200 ml (7 fl oz) milk

Sea buckthorn gel

500 ml (16 fl oz/1 pt) apple juice

200 g (7 oz) sea buckthorn (or passionfruit)

5 tbsp honey

100 g (3 oz) sugar

4 g (½ oz) agar agar

Rye bread chips

4 thin slices of rye bread

25 g (1 oz) English liquorice

50 g (2 oz) butter

Glazed carrots

12 small carrots, peeled

20 tarragon leaves, chopped

5 tbsp honey

50 ml (1⅔ fl oz) apple juice

Extra tarragon for decoration

Note: Any variety of passionfruit can be used instead of sea buckthorn

Sea buckthorn ice cream

Utensils: saucepan, spoon, strainer, whisk, ice cream machine

Bring the sea buckthorn, milk, cream, sugar and glucose to the boil and blend. Strain the mixture and bring it to the boil again. Pour over the egg yolks while whipping vigorously. Pour mixture back into the pot and thicken it gently over the heat. Set aside to cool, and then mix in an ice cream machine until frozen.

Carrot purée with sea buckthorn

Utensils: saucepan, blender, strainer, piping bag

Put all ingredients in a saucepan and boil for approximately 12–13 minutes until reduced by half. Blend mixture in a blender and then strain. Fill a piping bag with the mixture.

Sea buckthorn gel

Utensils: saucepan, spoon, strainer, form, knife

Bring juice, sea buckthorn, sugar and honey to the boil, then blend and strain. Add agar agar and boil for approximately 2 minutes. Pour mixture into a form. When set, cut the gel into small cubes.

Rye bread chips

Utensils: pastry brush, knife, baking tray, baking paper

Glaze the slices of rye bread with butter and grate liquorice on top. Place on a baking tray lined with baking paper and bake in a preheated oven for approximately 6 minutes at 175 °C (345 °F). Allow to cool so that they become crisp.

Glazed carrots

Utensils: saucepan, spoon

Put all ingredients in a saucepan and boil until the liquid has evaporated and the carrots are glazed.

Arrange the sea buckthorn ice cream on a plate, add the carrot purée with sea buckthorn and top with glazed carrots and sea buckthorn gel. Serve with ryebread chips.

sea buckthorn

Hippophae rhamnoides or sea buckthorn can be found in many places within Denmark. It is known as 'the passionfruit of the Nordic countries'. It can grow to 2–3 metres or higher provided it gets plenty of sunlight. The fruits are full of vitamin C and also contain vitamins A, B and E and are also suitable for making porridge and marmalade.

Aromatic dessert with flowers from the garden at Falsled Inn

200 ml (7 fl oz) cream
4 large rosehip flowers
50 g (2 oz) sugar
Juice of 1 lime
2 gelatine leaves

Rosengranitè
2 peony flowers
200 ml (7 fl oz) water
100 ml (4 fl oz) white wine
50 g (2 oz) sugar
Juice of 1 lime

Lavender ice cream
10 lavender flowers
1 tbsp Acacia honey
100 g (4 oz) sugar
250 ml (8 fl oz) milk
250 ml (8 fl oz) cream
5 egg yolks
Extra flowers for decoration

Blancmange of rosehips
Note: Start the day before.

Utensils: saucepan, bowl, strainer, spoon

Boil cream and sugar and then pour over the rosehips. Allow to cool and add the lime juice. Refrigerate overnight. The next day, strain the mixture and bring the liquid to the boil. Add the soaked gelatine, stir to dissolve and pour the mixture onto four dessert plates.

Rosengranitè
Note: Start the day before.

Utensils: saucepan, spoon, strainer, form, fork

Bring water, white wine, sugar and lime juice to the boil and then pour over the peonies. Set aside in a cool place and allow to infuse for 6 hours. Then strain, pour into a form and freeze. When frozen, use a fork to granulate.

Lavender ice cream
Note: Start the day before.

Utensils: saucepan, strainer, spoon, whisk, ice cream machine

Bring milk, cream, sugar and honey to the boil and then pour it over lavender. Refrigerate overnight. The next day, strain the mixture and bring the liquid to the boil. Pour the liquid over the egg yolks while whipping vigorously. Pour mixture back into the pot and thicken over the heat. Allow the mixture to cool; then mix in an ice cream machine until frozen.

Decorate with extra flowers.

Black September berries with hazelnuts

200 g (7 oz) strained blackberry purée

20 g (¾ oz) cornstarch

120 g (4 oz) egg whites

80 g (3 oz) sugar

Hazelnut snow

100 g (4 oz) malto

50 ml (1⅔ fl oz) hazelnut oil

Elderberry sorbet

500 g (16 oz/1lb) elderberries

100 g (4 oz) sugar

50 ml (1⅔ fl oz) glucose

Hazelnut parfait

500 ml (16 oz/1 pt) double cream

200 g (7 oz) chopped hazelnuts, without skin

150 g (5 oz) sugar

4 egg yolks

50 ml (1⅔ fl oz) hazelnut oil

Hazelnut/rye bread sprinkles

2 slices of rye bread

50 g (2 oz) hazelnuts

50 g (2 oz) cane sugar

Note: Prepare the soufflé the day before.

Blackberry soufflé

Utensils: 4 soufflé forms, saucepan, spoon, strainer, whisk, piping bag, knife

Begin by generously greasing four soufflé forms and then dusting them with sugar. Bring blackberries to the boil and add the cornstarch mixed with a little water to thicken the purée, boil for 2 minutes, strain and allow to cool. Whip the egg whites and sugar into a meringue and blend with the thickened purée. Fill piping bag with the mixture and pipe it into the soufflé forms, right to the edge. Use a knife to free the edges and freeze for 5 hours. Bake at 175 °C (345 °F) for 10 minutes. Serve immediately.

Hazelnut snow

Utensils: whisk, bowl

Whip the malto with the hazelnut oil until it has a snow-like consistency.

Elderberry sorbet

Utensils: saucepan, spoon, ice cream machine

Bring elderberries, sugar and glucose to the boil. Allow to cool; then mix in an ice cream machine until frozen.

Hazelnut parfait

Note: begin two days in advance

Utensils: toaster, bowl, strainer, whisk, blender, metal cylinder for freezing

Beginning two days in advance toast the hazelnuts until lightly golden, pour over the cream and allow to infuse in the fridge until the next day. Strain. Whip the hazelnut cream until it becomes light and foamy. Then whip the egg yolks, sugar and hazelnut oil until foamy. In a blender, mix everything together and freeze in a metal cylinder.

Hazelnut/rye bread sprinkles

Utensils: knife, baking tray, toaster, blender, metal cylinder for freezing

Cut the rye bread into slices and warm in a preheated oven at 80 °C (175 °F) until dry. Toast the hazelnuts until golden and pour everything into a blender with cane sugar. Blend to form sprinkles. When the parfait is frozen, remove it from metal cylinder to form logs and roll in sprinkles.

Place the blackberry soufflé on a plate, add the elderberry sorbet and top with hazelnut parfait and hazelnut snow. Serve with hazelnut ryebread sprinkles.

Raspberries with sheep's milk, red pepper and peaches

3 egg yolks

75 g (3 oz) sugar

200 g (7 oz) sheep's milk yoghurt

Juice and peel of 1 lemon

2 gelatine leaves

300 ml (10 fl oz/½ pt) cream, lightly whipped

Sorbet
150 g (5 oz) red pepper, cut into pieces

50 g (2 oz) sugar

125 g (4 oz) raspberries

50 ml (1⅔ fl oz) glucose

Juice of 1 lime

Preserved peaches
2 ripe peaches

200 ml (7 fl oz) water

200 ml (7 fl oz) sweet white wine

1 star anise

1 rosemary sprig

50 g (2 oz) honey

10 mint leaves

Juice and peel of 1 lemon

Decoration
20 raspberries

Spanish chervil

Sheep's milk mousse
Utensils: bowl, whisk

Whip egg yolks and sugar until smooth, turn the soaked gelatine into the yoghurt and combine this mixture with the egg mass. Then combine everything with the whipped cream.

Sorbet of red pepper and raspberries
Utensils: saucepan, strainer, ice cream machine

Boil all ingredients and blend, strain and allow to cool. Mix in an ice cream machine until frozen.

Preserved peaches
Utensils: saucepan, knife

Bring water, wine, herbs, honey, lemon peel and juice to the boil, cut peaches into halves and poach them in the liquid until tender. Allow to cool in the liquid. Cut peaches into slices when serving.

Decoration
Place the sheep's milk mousse on a plate, add the sorbet of red pepper and raspberries. Top with preserved peaches. Decorate the dessert with fresh raspberries and chervil.

raspberries

Raspberries contain vitamin C and iron. They are fine and aromatic berries often used in cakes, salads or as a dessert with ice cream or melon. They are most suitable for preserving and use in porridge.

Southern Jutland

A history of Southern Jutland coffee and cakes

ACCORDING TO INGE ADRIANSEN, curator and historian of Soenderborg Castle, 'Cakes of Southern Jutland' has been a stock phrase used by most Danes since reunification in 1920. The tradition of sumptuous cakes and desserts has flourished just as long in East and West Jutland, but the special reputation of 'the big cake table' of Southern Jutland is closely connected with the reunification of Denmark.

Until the middle of the 19th century, the people of Southern Jutland enjoyed their coffee and tea in peace and quiet when they met at inns. Around the 1850s coffee became standard and cakes were made on a frequent basis in the old stoves and iron ovens that were common at the time.

After 1864, when Southern Jutland became part of Germany, village halls were commonly built to accommodate gatherings that had formerly met in the local inns. Coffee and cakes were served and the participants brought their own home cooking, which filled a long table in the hall. There was a contest between the women regarding who could bake the most delicious and eye-catching cakes, tarts and layer tarts.

Before speeches or presentations were made, all the dishes were circulated in a steady stream. People could stack up the desserts on their plates and often there were just as many cakes as community songs sung. Their national spirit and the big cake table made a big impression on speakers visiting from Denmark. In the 1920s the bishop from Ribe in Southern Jutland said that the people of Southern Jutland had not two, but three sacraments: baptism, communion and cakes!

The big cake table was not only a phenomenon in the village halls, but also in private homes. It thrived at medium-sized farms where there was an abundance of eggs and cream. The traditional afternoon tea from Southern Jutland encompassed at least seven soft cakes and seven hard cakes.

Times change, and so do cooking traditions. Such large varieties of cakes are seldom consumed in the private home today, because of time pressures and the fact that people have become more aware of the benefits of a healthy lifestyle. Therefore, the full cake table has mostly disappeared but can still be seen in some form at certain inns and cafés in Southern Jutland.

Fakkelgaarden

" We are proud to work with local producers and use their fresh produce to pass on the food traditions from Southern Jutland in both classical and innovative ways "

Mikael Holm & Esben Krogh

FAKKELGAARDEN IS SITUATED in a beautiful region in Southern Jutland on the shores of Flensborg Fjord near the German border. The restaurant has received numerous awards for their excellent food, luxurious surroundings and exceptional service.

Young chefs Mikael Holm and Esben Krogh have brought to Fakkelgaarden solid experience and the ability to rediscover elements from Danish regional dishes and create their own style while still respecting traditions. They are known for making everything from scratch using local as well as international produce. Their priority is the use of organic ingredients. Many of the herbs and vegetables they use are grown in the garden at Fakkelgaarden and the cakes and desserts are made by a confectioner onsite. Their wine cellar is one of the finest in Denmark.

Fakkelgaarden has a network of suppliers who share their passion for gastronomy and raw produce. It is important for Holm and Krogh at Fakkelgaarden to maintain contact with local suppliers, of whom many have familial ties to the place. They also purchase produce from overseas suppliers, including truffles from Paris and cheese from Boulogne.

On the following pages Holm and Krogh bring together modern interpretations of local specialities. Krog has previously worked for the Michelin-star restaurant Kong Hans Kælder and two-Michelin-star Kommandanten in Copenhagen as well as for Christies in Southern Jutland and three-Michelin-star Auberges de Lill in France. He is an avid collector of wine and has a special interest in the Alsace region of France. Mikael Holm also gained experience at the prestigious Christies in Southern Jutland and at Restaurant Marie Louise owned by Michel Michaud. In Sydney, Australia he studied wine and developed a passion for and knowledge of Australian and New Zealand wines.

The buildings of Fakkelgaarden were originally the setting for 'Grænsehjemmet', which means 'Home of the Border', a combined youth hostel and cultural house for young people from the northern region of Schleswig and other parts of old Denmark. It was also established to improve visitors' knowledge of the border-country, thereby achieving a greater understanding of the area's unique culture. The name Fakkelgaarden refers to the ever-burning fireplace in front of the restaurant's entry. Today the hotel, which is located in an entirely renovated building that opened in 1992, is owned by the Fleggaard family.

Blue cheese from Southern Jutland and rye bread, red onion rings, gel and cress

250 ml (8 fl oz) full-cream milk

250 ml (8 fl oz) double cream

165 g (6 oz) blue cheese

Juice of ½ lemon

2 gelatine leaves

Ground salt and pepper

1 bunch of asparagus

Butter and salt for steaming

1 leek

Pepper

20 ml (⅔ fl oz) vinaigrette

Chiffon of cheese with green asparagus and burnt leeks

Accompaniment: rye bread, red onion rings, gel and cress

Utensils: saucepan, bowl blender, spoon, peeling knife, baking tray

Warm the milk and double cream in a saucepan. Soak the gelatine in cold water for 5 minutes, remove and squeeze to remove excess water, then add the warm milk. Pour the mixture into a blender with the whole piece of cheese and blend until smooth. Add the lemon juice and add salt and pepper to taste. Set aside in a cool place.

Steam the green asparagus in a little water, butter and salt until lightly tender. Peel a couple of asparagus spears lengthwise. Marinate the slivers in vinaigrette. Clean the leek and bake in a preheated oven at 180 °C (350 °F) until it is completely dry and charred, approximately 20 minutes. Process the leek to a fine powder.

Place the chiffon of blue cheese on rye bread, decorate with green asparagus, red onion rings, gel and cress. Sprinkle the powdered leek over the dish.

mould cheese

Mould cheese is a soft cheese made from cow's or goat's milk. There are two varieties:
1. *Very ripe, mild white cheeses such as Camembert or Brie. They are matured for approximately two weeks to three months.*
2. *Blue cheeses such as Danablu, Gorgonzola, Roquefort and Stilton are matured for up to six months or sometimes more.*

In this recipe Fakkelgaarden uses Ask cheese, which is from a small dairy in Western Jutland called Troldhede.

Cheese with honey

175 g (6 oz) hard cheese

Honey

Buttered toasted rye bread

Wood sorrel (or a herb like chervil or sage)

Preserved walnuts
200 g (7 oz) walnuts

375 ml (½ bottle/ 12 fl oz) red wine

100 ml (4 fl oz) orange juice

¼ orange, sliced

½ vanilla pod

200 g (7 oz) brown sugar

35 g (1 oz) honey

Utensils: knife, toaster

Cut the hard cheese into thin flakes. Drizzle a few lines of honey across the cheese, crush preserved walnuts and wood sorrel and sprinkle over the top. Serve with toasted and buttered slices of rye bread.

Preserved walnuts
Utensils: saucepan, knife

Blanch the walnuts in plenty of water. Blend the rest of the ingredients and bring to the boil. Add walnuts and boil until the texture is like syrup. Store in a container or airtight jar.

Traditional bread layer cake from Southern Jutland

6 eggs

250 g (8 oz) sugar

100 g (4 oz) shredded rye bread

1 tsp baking powder

100 g (4 oz) chopped nuts

Filling
500 ml (16 fl oz/1 pt) double cream, for whipping

Homemade blackcurrant jam

Decoration
Whipped cream

70 g (2 oz) toasted, chopped hazelnuts

70 g (2 oz) chopped dark chocolate

Utensils: bowl, whisk, blender, three layer cake forms, butter for the cake forms

Filling
Separate the eggs and whip the whites until very stiff. Slowly add the sugar. Add the egg yolks one at a time. Gradually blend in the shredded rye bread, baking powder and nuts. Spread the dough into three layer-cake forms greased with butter. Bake the layers in a preheated oven at 220 °C (430 °F) for approximately 10 minutes.

Decoration
Whip the double cream until stiff. Spread chocolate and blackcurrant jam on the bottom layer, add the second layer and spread with whipped cream. Top with the remaining layer and decorate with whipped cream, hazelnuts and chopped chocolate.

Apple cake

6 eating apples

250 g (8 oz) sugar

1 vanilla pod

100 g (4 oz) rye breadcrumbs

25 g (1 oz) butter

75 g (3 oz) crushed macaroons

300 ml (10 fl oz/½ pt) double cream

Berry gel*

Utensils: peeling knife, saucepan, spoon, glass bowl

Peel and core the apples, cut them into quarters and boil with the sugar, vanilla pod and a little water until this becomes a compote. Toast the rye breadcrumbs in a pan with the butter. Allow to cool, then mix with the crushed macaroons. When the apple compote is cold, put it into a glass bowl layered with the rye breadcrumbs and finally the lightly whipped cream. Top the cake with the berry gel.

*Berry gel can be made from 200 millilitres (7 fluid ounces) of fruit juice from strawberries, cherries or raspberries, two gelatine sheets and a little sugar. Place the gelatine in a bowl over a warm water bath and mix in the fruit juice until the gelatine has dissolved. Add sugar. Remove from the heat and allow to cool.

Alternatively, any fresh berries that are in season can replace the berry gel.

Juice blancmange with cream sauce and redcurrants

300 ml (10 fl oz/½ pt) redcurrant juice

50 g (2 oz) sugar

2 egg whites

8 gelatine leaves

Crème sauce

2 egg yolks

2½ tbsp sugar

200 ml (7 fl oz) cream

200 ml (7 fl oz) double cream

Seeds from ½ vanilla pod

Utensils: bowl, saucepan, spoon, blender

Soak the gelatine in cold water for about 8 minutes. Remove the gelatine from the water and squeeze to remove the excess water. Then place the gelatine in a bowl over a warm water bath and mix in the redcurrant juice until the gelatine has dissolved. Remove from the heat. In a bowl, mix the gelatine and the redcurrant juice until gelatine has dissolved.

Blend the egg whites until stiff and turn in the sugar. Pour the redcurrant juice in the egg whites and mix them together slowly. Set aside to cool until set.

Traditional crème sauce (from the old days)

Utensils: whisk, bowl, saucepan, blender, spoon

Whip the egg yolks and sugar until light and fluffy. Bring cream and seeds from the vanilla pod to the boil and then blend the warm cream with the egg mass while stirring. Whip it together while warming over a low heat until it has thickened. The cream must not boil. Remove from heat and stir a few times. Whip the double cream until stiff. Add the stiffly whipped cream and stir thoroughly before serving.

Serve the cream sauce as an accompaniment to the juice blancmange. Decorate with redcurrant.

Spelt rice with lemon and cherries

100 g (4 oz) spelt rice

500 ml (16 fl oz/1 pt) whole milk

75 g (3 oz) sugar

1 vanilla pod

25 g (1 oz) dried cherries

200 ml (7 fl oz) cream

Grated peel and juice of 1 lemon

Cherry compote
200 g (7 oz) cherries

100 g (4 oz) sugar

100 ml (4 fl oz) water or cherry juice

A little lemon juice (optional)

Utensils: bowl, saucepan, spoon, whisk

Wash the spelt rice in cold water. Place in a saucepan with milk and boil for approximately 20 minutes until tender. Add sugar, vanilla and dried cherries and let it simmer for 5 minutes or more. Remove from heat and add lemon peel and juice. Set aside in a cool place. Whisk the double cream and add the cooled spelt rice. Continue to whisk until soft and creamy in texture.

Fresh cherry compote
Utensils: peeler/paring knife, saucepan

Pit the fresh cherries and boil with water and sugar until they are tender. Allow to cool and add a little lemon juice to taste if required.

spelt rice (perlespelt)

Derived from wheat, spelt rice is a traditional farmer's food that has recently had a renaissance in Denmark and is now used in both traditional and modern dishes. It originates from the Mediterranean region, where legend has it that the Roman legionnaires survived on spelt rice during their long expeditions. Its use can be traced back more than 5000 years to the Mesopotamians, who believed spelt rice maintained a strong body and healthy blood. Scientists have proved that spelt rice is rich in vitamins, minerals and essential amino acids. The spelt rice used by Fakkelgaarden is from Skaertoft Mill in Augustenborg, Southern Jutland.

Buttermilk mousse with fresh strawberries

200 g (7 oz) fresh strawberries

100 g (4 oz) sugar

3 eggs

220 g (8 oz) buttermilk

½ gelatine leaf

200 g (7 oz) double cream

Grated peel and juice of ½ lemon

Rye bread ice cream

1 l (2 pt) organic full-cream milk

250 ml (8 fl oz) egg yolks

325 g (11 oz) brown sugar

4 slices of rye bread

1 tsp of malt flour

Crisp rye bread

200 ml (7 fl oz) water

200 ml (7 fl oz) sugar

Utensils: bowl, whisk, saucepan, spoon

Marinate fresh strawberries by adding 25 grams (1 ounce) of sugar. Whisk egg with the remaining 75 grams (3 ounces) of sugar until light and fluffy. In a saucepan warm the lemon juice over low heat. Soak the gelatine in water for 5 minutes, then remove and squeeze to remove the excess water. Melt the gelatine in the warm lemon juice. Allow the gelatine and lemon juice mixture to cool a little before pouring it over the buttermilk. Blend the buttermilk mixture with the egg mass and lightly whipped cream. Arrange the strawberries on the bottom of the plates and pour the buttermilk mousse over the top.

Rye bread ice cream

Utensils: saucepan, spoon, ice cream machine

Bring the milk to the boil and thicken with the egg yolks. Add brown sugar. Break the rye bread into small pieces and toast until crisp and crumbly in the oven. Blend the mixture with breadcrumbs until smooth. Mix in an ice cream machine.

Crisp rye bread

Utensils: knife, pastry brush, baking tray, baking paper

Cut some rye bread (a couple of days old is ideal) into thin slices and cut these into egg-size shapes. Glaze with the sugar brine*, place on a baking tray lined with baking paper and bake in a preheated oven at 180 °C (350 °F) until golden and crisp.

Arrange the buttermilk mousse in portions on a plate with rye bread ice cream and crisp rye bread.

*Sugar brine is made with an equal ratio of sugar to water

Good advice (Gode råd)

75 g (3 oz) butter

100 g (4 oz) icing sugar or sugar, sifted

100 ml (4 fl oz) coffee creamer

125 g (4 oz) plain flour

3 egg whites, whipped until stiff

Utensils: waffle iron, whisk, bowl, pastry brush, wooden spoon

Mix the butter and sugar with the cream until smooth. Add the flour and finally the whipped egg whites. Glaze the waffle iron with a little oil and butter. Spoon 1 tablespoon of the batter onto the waffle iron. Close the iron and bake for only a couple of minutes until the cookie is light golden and crisp. Repeat until all of the batter is used.

To serve: Bend the newly baked cookies over the shaft of a wooden spoon, so they can be filled with whipped cream.

Lard cakes (Fedtkager)

350 g (12 oz) lard

50 g (2 oz) butter

375 g (13 oz) sugar

750 g (26 oz) flour

1 tsp of vanilla sugar

1 tsp of ammonium bicarbonate

65 g (2 oz) cocoa

Utensils: bowl, whisk, baking tray, baking paper

Knead all ingredients into a homogenous mass. Place the dough in the fridge for about an hour. Roll dough into small balls and bake them on a baking tray lined with baking paper in the middle of the oven at 220 °C (430 °F) for approximately 12 minutes.

Jewish cakes (Jødekager)

200 g (7 oz) butter

250 g (8 oz) flour

120 g (4 oz) sugar

½ tsp ammonium bicarbonate

2 eggs (1 for brushing)

To decorate
Almond slivers and cane sugar

Utensils: bowl, whisk, rolling pin

Knead all ingredients into a homogeneous mass. Roll a sausage measuring 4 centimetres in diameter. Refrigerate for a minimum of 3 hours. Cut 5-millimetre slices. Sprinkle the slices with almond slivers and cane sugar and bake at 180 °C (350 °F) for approximately 10 minutes.

Carl Christian Nissen

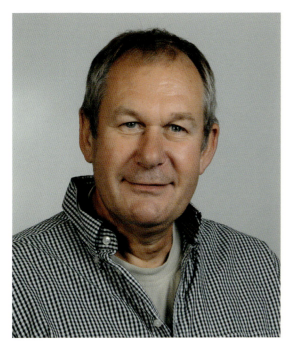

> *The recipe is one thing. How you interpret the recipe and treat the raw materials – that is quite another thing, and can make all the difference*
>
> Carl Christian Nissen

SOME OF THE SWEETEST MEMORIES from my upbringing in Sønderborg are of the frequent visits to Calle's Bakery with a bunch of friends after school, in the early hours of Saturday morning after a night out, or on Sunday mornings. There was always an excuse to walk those extra miles to get some delicious pastries directly from the oven.

For more than 30 years Carl Christian Nissen and his wife Grete owned and managed Calle's Bakery in Sønderborg in Southern Jutland. He is very proficient baker and he has kindly provided three of the most popular recipes from his bakery.

Throughout his childhood Nissen's family often enjoyed the "Cakes of Southern Jutland", a practice that dates from when the region was under German rule. This tradition involved 16 different home-baked cakes, all of which had to be tasted in order not to insult the hostess. Without a doubt it was this baking tradition that awakened his passion for this exciting profession.

Over the years Carl Christian Nissen made a fragilité cake, which was very popular and delivered to many bakeries in Denmark. The recipe was a secret for all those years until now. He has disclosed the recipe especially for this book. It is a delicious cake, which with its spongy and soft texture differs from other fragilité cakes.

Carl Christian Nissen was born in Southern Jutland and has worked as a baker since 1969. He sold his bakery in 2007 and has since worked as a specialist baker at Alsion, a magnificent new centre for research, culture and innovation in Sønderborg in Southern Jutland.

Fragilité

The fragilité cake is served topped with fruit and ice cream as a dessert.

400 g (14 oz) raw marzipan
420 g (15 oz) egg whites
500 g (16 oz/1 lb) sugar
180 g (6 oz) icing sugar
180 g (6 oz) chopped hazelnuts

Utensils: bowl, knife, whisk, four spring forms measuring 22 centimeters in diameter, spatula, baking tray, baking paper

Add a bit of the egg whites to the marzipan to make it soft. In a bowl, mix egg whites and sugar until just stiff. Add the icing sugar and whip for another 30 seconds.

Blend in the hazelnuts and pour the mixture into four spring forms, each measuring 22 centimetres in diameter. Spread out the mass and sprinkle with hazelnuts.

Place on a baking tray lined with baking paper in a preheated oven at 155–160 °C (310–320 °F) for approximately 45–50 minutes.

The fragilité layers should fall down a little in the middle when they are removed from the oven.

Dannebrog canapé
(Dannebrogsnitte)

Calle's Bakery had a specialty called Dannebrog (the Danish flag) canapé, named after the Danish flag Dannebrog, consisting of red and white marzipan on top. It is an easy cake to make. This canapé originates from the traditional raspberry canapé (Hindbærsnitte).

280 g (10 oz) plain flour
200 g (7 oz) butter
100 g (4 oz) icing sugar
1 egg
1 pinch (less than ½ tsp) baking powder
1 pinch (less than ½ tsp) vanilla
Raspberry jam

Decoration
Approximately 100 g (4 oz) icing sugar
Approximately 1–2 tbsp boiling water
100 g (4 oz) marzipan
Red food dye

Utensils: bowl, whisk, rolling pin, knife, spatula, baking tray, baking paper

Combine all the ingredients carefully. Place the mixture in a cool place for approximately 1–2 hours. Then roll the dough to 2.5 millimetres in thickness and cut into two equally long and wide squares.

Bake on a baking tray lined with baking paper in a preheated oven at 200 °C (390 °F) for approximately 10–12 minutes until the squares become golden brown.

While the dough is still warm, spread raspberry jam onto one of the squares, then place the other square on top of the jam like a sandwich. Allow to cool.

Decoration

Blend icing sugar and water to a suitable texture.

Spread a thin layer of the icing sugar mixture on top of the canapé. Add red food dye to half of the marzipan. Then spread a thin layer of white marzipan and cross with strips of red marzipan. Cut into appropriate sizes.

Gallop pretzel (Galopkringle)

40 g (1 oz) yeast

40 g (1 oz) sugar

½ tsp salt

2 eggs

175 ml (6 fl oz) milk

350 g (12 oz) butter

500 g (16 oz/1 lb) wheat flour

Marzipan blend

150 g (5 oz) raw marzipan

150 g (5 oz) butter

150 g (5 oz) brown sugar

Raisins (optional)

Decoration

1 egg, lightly whipped

Hazelnut flakes

Sugar

Yeast dough
Utensils: saucepan, whisk, bowl

Dissolve the yeast in the milk until it is lukewarm. Melt the butter and mix it with the other ingredients. Knead the dough thoroughly until it is smooth.

Marzipan blend
Utensils: bowl, blender

Blend the marzipan with the butter and brown sugar.

Decoration
Utensils: whisk, rolling pin, knife, spatula, baking tray, baking paper, pastry brush

On a well-floured bench or table, roll out the dough and cut it into two equal pieces. Fill each piece with the marzipan blend. Fold one of the long edges to the middle of the piece, then fold the other edge towards the middle as well to cover marzipan filling. Press the dough lightly.

Place the dough on a baking tray lined with baking paper. Form the dough into a pretzel shape by pressing the ends of the two pieces of dough together.

Set aside the dough to rise for approximately 45 minutes to an hour (the dough must rise to double its original size). Then glaze with egg and sprinkle with sugar and chopped hazelnuts. Bake the pretzels in a preheated oven at 200 °C (390 °F) for approximately 20 minutes.

The gallop pretzel-shaped pastry is a specialty from Southern Jutland. It was once a common feature on the big cake tables of Southern Jutland. It is still a hugely popular pastry, especially when unexpected visitors drop by, because it is easy to make and it is ready very quickly – which is why it is called a gallop pastry!

Mid Jutland

Restaurant Frederikshøj

> *The restaurant is like the Royal Theatre. When you enter the theatre all your experiences and events during the evening are taken care of*
>
> Palle Enevoldsen

PALLE ENEVOLDSEN has long been one of the most awarded chefs and highly regarded food judges in Denmark. He established the classic gourmet restaurant Frederikshøj in Århus in 2006. For more than 20 years he has challenged the ideas of the classical kitchen. At the age of 26 he opened his first restaurant and later worked for Falsled Kro (see page 74). He went on to establish Restaurant Le Canard in Århus, which he managed for 12 years and was awarded 'Restaurant of the Year'.

Frederikshøj is situated in beautiful surroundings and its association with food dates back to 1816 when the forester living in the house served coffee to guests in order to earn extra income. The place is now completely refurbished with a large glazed section that provides a splendid view across the park and bay. The restaurant seats approximately 200 guests and although the interior is elegant and contemporary in style (designed by Enevoldsen's wife, designer Marianne Probst Enevoldsen) the space remains cosy and welcoming for guests.

CHEF WASSIM HALLAL became a partner in August 2009 and has forged an equally brilliant career. Hallal is known as the 'Gastronomic Volcano'. He previously owned his own restaurant, which was awarded 'Restaurant of the Year'. Hallal was born in Lebanon and moved to Denmark with his parents in 1984, settling in Thy in Northern Jutland. His father was also a chef and his mother was a food stylist. Hallal worked in a two-Michelin-star restaurant in Belgium and returned to Denmark to work as a head chef for Molskroen near Aarhus from 2003–2006. Molskroen also became a 'Restaurant of the Year'.

Palle Enevoldsens' style is French cuisine whereas Wassim Hallal is innovative and meticulous, and together they provide their guests with a sublime experience.

Apple with chocolate cake

100 ml (4 fl oz) apple juice

100 g (4 oz) sugar

Seeds from ½ vanilla pod

2 apples

Nut layer
2 eggs

50 g (2 oz) sugar

40 g (1 oz) plain flour

30 g (1 oz) nut flour

1 g (⅛ oz) baking powder

White chocolate cream
1 gelatine leaf

100 ml (4 fl oz) double cream

30 g (1 oz) white chocolate

Preserved apple cubes of 2 apples (see above)

Apple mousse
100 ml (4 fl oz) apple juice

2 ml (⅛ fl oz) lemon juice

1 g (⅛ oz) agar agar

1 gelatine leaf

100 ml (4 fl oz) double cream

25 g (1 oz) pasteurised egg whites

20 g (1 oz) sugar

Note: Start recipe the day before.

Preserved apples
Utensils: saucepan, peeling knife, knife, bowl

Bring apple juice, sugar and vanilla to the boil. Peel the apples, cut them into 1-centimetre cubes and mix them into the sugar syrup. Set aside in a cool place until the following day.

Nut layer
Utensils: whisk, bowl, baking tray, spoon, blender, 18-centimeter ring for cutting out the layer, baking tray, baking paper

Whip the eggs. Warm the sugar in the oven at 170 °C (340 °F) for about 5 minutes and then whip into the eggs. Sift the wheat flour with the baking powder and combine with the nut flour. Blend the egg mass at high speed, then carefully blend in the flour.

Spread a 1-centimetre layer of the mixture in a baking tray with baking paper. Bake at 170 °C (340 °F) for approximately 9 minutes. Use an 18-centimetre ring to cut out the layer.

White chocolate cream
Utensils: bowl, saucepan, spoon

Soften the gelatine in cold water, remove from water and squeeze out the excess water. In a saucepan warm the gelatine with the double cream over low heat. Mix the chocolate into the double cream and fold the preserved apple cubes into the mixture.

Place the nut layer in an 18-centimetre serving ring. Sprinkle with a little syrup from the apples. Pour in the white chocolate. Allow to cool.

Apple mousse
Utensils: saucepan, blender, whisk, bowl, cake ring approximately 20 centimentre in diameter

Bring apple juice and lemon juice to the boil with agar agar. Cool the syrup until it has set and then blend it until smooth.

Soften the gelatine in cold water and then mix it with the double cream. Whip the egg whites and sugar until stiff. Mix the blended apple syrup with the cream and gently fold it into the stiffly whipped eggs.

Pour the apple mousse into the spring form, then add the white chocolate cream and place it back in the fridge. This forms the centre of the cake.

When the three layers have settled, remove the ring and place a larger ring (approximately 20 centimetres in diameter) around the cake. It should be a taller ring, so that you can form a layer around the cake.

Chocolate mousse

200 ml (7 fl oz) double cream

3 gelatine leaves

150 g (5 oz) chocolate (70 percent cocoa)

30 g (1 oz) pasteurised egg whites

20 g (¾ oz) sugar

Chocolate gel

30 ml (1 fl oz) water

30 g (1 oz) sugar

10 g (½ oz) cocoa

20 ml (⅔ fl oz) whipped cream

½ gelatine leaf

Chocolate plates

300 g (10 oz) chocolate (70 percent cocoa)

Chocolate mousse
Utensils: bowl, spoon, blender, spatula

Dissolve the gelatine in cold water for 5 minutes, then remove the gelatine and squeeze to remove the excess water. In a saucepan heat the double cream at low heat and combine it with the gelatine. Mix until the gelatine has dissolved. Then add the chocolate and stir to combine.

Blend the egg whites and sugar until stiff and then gently fold the mixture into the chocolate and double cream mass. Cover the cake with the chocolate mousse. Shake the form a little in order to avoid air bubbles and set it aside again in a cool place.

Chocolate gel
Utensils: saucepan, bowl, spoon

Bring the water, sugar and cocoa to the boil. Soak the gelatine in cold water for 5 minutes, squeeze to remove the excess water, then combine it with the whipped cream until dissolved. Mix the cocoa blend and cream together and allow to cool. Before it sets, carefully pour the mixture over the cake and place it back in the fridge.

Chocolate plates
Utensils: bowl, saucepan, spoon, piece of plastic, knife

Bring 200 grams of chocolate to 45 °C (110 °F) over a water bath. Chop 100 grams of chocolate and blend it into the melted chocolate immediately after it has been taken off the heat. Spread a thin layer of the chocolate on a piece of plastic. Just before the chocolate sets, cut it into plates, their length matching the height of the cake.

Remove the cake from the ring and the baking tray. Remove the baking paper. Place the chocolate pieces around the cake before serving.

> *Work for what you are passionate about and don't feel sorry for yourself. Don't look back until you have reached your goal*
>
> Wassim Hallal

Coffee and mascarpone cake

100 g (4 oz) pasteurised eggs

100 g (4 oz) sugar

40 g (2 oz) wheat flour

1 g (⅛ oz) baking powder

50 g (2 oz) nut flour

Mascarpone
200 g (7 oz) mascarpone

100 g (4 oz) icing sugar

90 g (3 oz) pasteurised egg yolks

Seeds from 1 vanilla pod

20 ml (¾ fl oz) rum

10 ml (½ fl oz) lemon juice

100 ml (4 fl oz) strong coffee

3 gelatine leaves

100 ml (4 fl oz) double cream

Decoration
50 g (2 oz) cocoa

Nut layer
Utensils: strainer, bowl, food mixer, spoon, spatula, baking tray, baking paper

Sift the flour and the baking powder and mix together with the nut flour.

In a food mixer whip the eggs and sugar to the highest possible volume and then gently stir in the flour.

Spread a layer of the mixture, approximately 1 centimetre thick, onto a baking tray lined with baking paper. Place it in a preheated oven at 170 °C (340 °F) for approximately 13 minutes.

Mascarpone
Utensils: whisk, bowl, food mixer, spoon, 15-centimetre square tin that is approximately 7 centimetres high, spatula

Whip the mascarpone until smooth and even. In a food mixer blend the icing sugar, vanilla seeds and egg yolks until light and fluffy.

Soften the gelatine in cold water for 5 minutes, squeeze to remove excess water, and then combine with rum, lemon juice and most of the strong coffee until dissolved. Lightly whip the cream and fold it into the mascarpone. Gradually blend the mixture of gelatine and rum with the fluffy egg mass. Then combine the egg mass with the mascarpone and the double cream.

Cut the cake with a 15-centimetre square cake tin that is approximately 7 centimetres high.

Sprinkle the rest of the coffee over the layers. Place one layer in the cake ring. Spread half of the cream on the layer in the ring, place the other layer carefully on top and cover with the rest of the cream. Refrigerate until the cream has settled.

Decoration
Sprinkle the cake with a thin layer of cocoa, remove the cake ring and arrange on a serving plate.

Strawberry and orange cake

100 g (4 oz) pasteurised eggs

50 g (2 oz) sugar

40 g (2 oz) wheat flour

1 g (⅛ oz) baking powder

Grated peel from 2 well-washed oranges

Strawberry mousse
350 g (12 oz) fresh strawberries

250 ml (8 fl oz) cream, lightly whipped

5 gelatine leaves

50 g (2 oz) pasteurised egg whites

50 g (2 oz) sugar

Orange soufflé
300 ml (10 fl oz) freshly squeezed orange juice

3 g (¼ oz) agar agar

75 g (3 oz) sugar

Seeds of ½ vanilla pod

4 gelatine leaves

50 ml (2 fl oz) Cointreau

300 ml (10 fl oz) cream, lightly whipped

50 g (2 oz) fresh strawberries

Cake layers
Utensils: peeling knife, blender, strainer, 18-centimetre cake ring, baking paper, spatula, knife

Blend the eggs and sugar. Sift the flour and baking powder and blend with grated orange peel. Blend the egg mass to its maximum volume and then carefully blend in the flour.

Fill an 18-centimetre cake ring lined with baking paper and bake at 160 °C (320 °F) for approximately 14 minutes.

When the cake has cooled, cut it horizontally to create two round layers.

Strawberry mousse
Note: keep some of the strawberries for decoration, choosing strawberries that are similar in size.

Utensils: blender, bowl, whisk, spoon, 18-centimetre cake ring

Blend approximately 300 grams (10 ounces) of the strawberries.

Soften the gelatine in cold water for 5 minutes, squeeze to remove excess water and dissolve it with the blended strawberries. Whip the egg whites and sugar until stiff. Gradually add the lightly whipped cream to the strawberries. Then, fold in the stiffly whipped egg whites.

Put one of the cake layers inside an 18-centimetre cake ring and pour over the mousse. Place the other cake layer on top and refrigerate until settled.

Orange soufflé
Utensils: saucepan, blender, bowl, knife, whisk, 20-centimetre cake ring, baking paper

Bring the orange juice to the boil with agar agar, sugar and vanilla seeds. Set aside the syrup in a cool place until it has set. Then blend it to a smooth purée.

Soften the gelatine in cold water for 5 minutes, squeeze to remove excess water and combine it with the Cointreau. Chop the strawberries into squares.

Combine the gelatine and Cointreau mixture with the purée, then add the lightly whipped cream and stir until combined.

Line a 20-centimetre cake ring with baking paper. Take the cake out of the fridge and remove the ring. Place the cake in the middle of the larger lined cake ring, and sprinkle the chopped strawberries on top. Pour the orange soufflé over the cake and place it in the fridge again. It is important that the orange mousse covers the cake completely. Shake the cake a little, to avoid air bubbles. When the cake has set, remove the ring and decorate the cake with slices of strawberries.

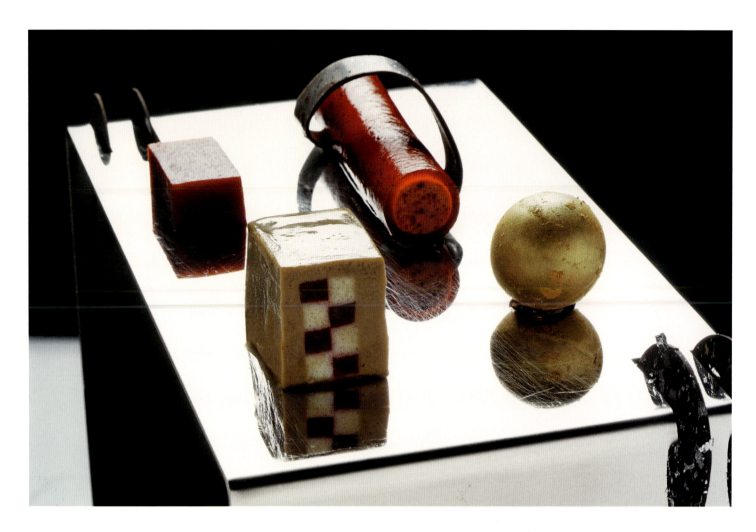

Cherries and chocolate cake

100 g (4 oz) pasteurised eggs

50 g (2 oz) sugar

30 g (1 oz) wheat flour

20 g (¾ oz) cocoa

1 g (⅛ oz) baking powder

50 g (2 oz) hazelnuts

50 g (2 oz) pistachios

Preserved cherries

250 g (8 oz) fresh cherries

30 ml (1 fl oz) Pernod

30 ml (1 fl oz) water

75 g (3 oz) sugar

Seeds from ½ vanilla pod

Note: Start the preserved cherries the day before.

Bunde (cake layer)
Utensils: food mixer, bowl, sieve, spoon, spatula, baking tray, baking paper

Using a food mixer, whip the eggs and sugar until light and fluffy. Sift flour, baking powder and cocoa together. When the egg mass has been whipped to its highest possible volume, carefully blend in the flour mix. Spread a 1–1.5 centimetre layer onto a baking tray lined with baking paper. Sprinkle with chopped nuts and bake at 170 °C (340 °F) for 9 minutes.

Preserved cherries
Utensils: peeling knife, saucepan, spoon

Pit the cherries. Bring Pernod, water and sugar to the boil. Add the vanilla seeds and cherries. Infuse the cherries in the syrup until the next day.

Cherry squares

200 ml (7 fl oz) cherry juice

60 g (2 oz) sugar

Seeds from ¼ vanilla pod

2 g (⅛ oz) of agar agar

Cherry mousse

2 gelatine leaves

20 ml (⅔ fl oz) Pernod

100 g (4 oz) cherry gel purée (see cherry squares recipe above)

25 g (1 oz) pasteurised egg whites

25 g (1 oz) sugar

100 ml (4 fl oz) double cream

Chocolate mousse

2 gelatine leaves

200 ml (7 fl oz) double cream

65 g (2 oz) chocolate (70 percent cocoa)

25 g (1 oz) pasteurised egg whites

25 g (1 oz) sugar

Decoration

300 g (10 oz) chocolate (70 percent cocoa)

90 g (3 oz) cocoa butter

Chocolate ganache

100 ml (4 fl oz) double cream

20 g (¾ oz) glucose

100 g (4 oz) chocolate

Chocolate tubes

5 g chocolate (¼ oz) (70 percent cocoa)

Cherry squares
Utensils: spoon, saucepan, small form, knife

Combine cherry juice, sugar, vanilla seeds and agar agar in a saucepan and bring to the boil while stirring. Boil for 30 seconds, then take off the heat.

Pour the boiled syrup into a small form to a height of 2 centimetres and set aside in a cool place until it sets.

Purée half of the gel (to be used in the cherry mousse recipe below) and cut the rest into small squares to be used as a decoration.

Cherry mousse
Utensils: bowl, spoon, blender, cake ring or baking tray, baking paper, strainer, spatula

Soak the gelatine in cold water for 5 minutes, squeeze to remove excess water, then combine it with 20 millilitres of Pernod and the cherry purée. Whisk the egg whites and sugar until stiff. Fold the whipped cream into the cherry purée and then carefully fold this mixture into the stiffly whipped egg whites.

To assemble: Cut two layers of the cake using a cake ring lined with baking paper measuring approximately 15 centimetres in diameter or cut the cake into 15- by 15-centimetre squares. Place one of the layers in the bottom of the cake ring or on a baking tray lined with baking paper. Strain the preserved cherries and spread half the quantity on the bottom layer. Then spread half the cherry mousse on top of this. Place the other layer on top of the cherry mousse. Add a touch of the syrup from the preserved cherries to the layer. Place the rest of the preserved cherries on top of the cake layer and cover with the rest of the cherry mousse. This is the centre of the cake. Refrigerate for approximately 20 minutes until the mouse has set.

Chocolate mousse
Utensils: bowl, saucepan, spoon, blender, cake ring measuring approximately 16 centimetres, baking paper

Soften the gelatine in cold water for 5 minutes, squeeze to remove excess water. In a saucepan warm the double cream over low heat, add the gelatine and stir until melted. Add the chocolate into the warm double cream. Mix the chocolate and cream until smooth. Blend the egg whites and sugar until stiff and fold gently into the chocolate mixture. The mousse is now ready to be poured into the cake.

Remove the cake from the fridge and remove the ring. Line a bigger cake ring (of approximately 16 centimetres) with baking paper and place the cake in the middle of the ring. Cover with the chocolate mousse and refrigerate for approximately 1 hour. It might be necessary to shake the cake gently in order to avoid air bubbles forming on the sides.

Decoration
Utensils: saucepan, spoon, spray pistol

In a saucepan, melt the chocolate with the cocoa butter. Take the cake out of the freezer and remove the ring. Pour the chocolate mixture into a spray pistol and spray the cake with a thin layer of chocolate.

Chocolate ganache
Utensils: saucepan, knife, spoon, piping bag

In a saucepan, bring the double cream and glucose to boiling point. Chop the chocolate, blend it with the warm cream to a smooth texture. Place the ganache in a piping bag.

Chocolate tubes
Utensils: saucepan, knife, spoon, 2 pieces of plastic, spatula

Melt 50 grams (2 ounces) of the chocolate to 45° C (110° F). Take it off the heat. Then chop the rest of the chocolate and blend with the warm chocolate.

Cut a piece of plastic measuring 5 centimetres wide and 10 centimetres long. Use a spatula to spread a thin layer of chocolate on the plastic. When the chocolate starts to stiffen, cut it into long rows. Twist the chocolate to form tubes. Place in the fridge.

Decorate the cake with three small dots of the chocolate ganache. Place small squares of the cherry gel on the cake. Finally, remove the plastic from the chocolate tubes and place them on top of the cake.

Northern Jutland

Ruths Restaurant, Skagen

> *There are no alternatives or compromises when it comes to ensuring an optimal taste sensation always*
>
> Michel Michaud

RUTHS HOTEL IS SITUATED in Gl. Skagen, 4 kilometres south of Skagen, among the beautiful white beaches and unspoilt environment at the northern tip of Denmark in Northern Jutland. The light is very special in this region and the characteristic yellow houses with whitewashed rooftops and famous sand dunes have attracted thousands of visitors over the years.

Ruths Hotel was originally a bathhouse and guesthouse and was built by Emma and Hans Christian Ruth in 1904. In 2003 J Philip-Sørensen bought Ruths Hotel and today it is one of the most beautiful hotels in Denmark and a cosy rendezvous point (*hygge* in Danish) for visitors.

Since 2004 Michel Michaud has been the executive chef of Ruths Gourmet and Ruths Brasserie at Ruths Hotel. He has received the prestigious Danish 'Chefs Award' from The Foundation for the Advancement of Danish Gastronomy – the winner of which is chosen by hundreds of leading chefs in Denmark. Michaud shows an uncompromising engagement with his trade. He presents the 'now' with a view to the past. The cuisine is distinctively French and of sublime quality. Nothing is left to chance; all produce is checked by Michel Michaud himself.

Michel Michaud has made a significant impact on Danish gastronomy. In 1971 he came to Denmark from Bretagne in France when he was asked to manage Falsled Kro (see page 74). He introduced French cuisine to Denmark and started a revolution within Danish gastronomy. In 1976 he moved to the award-winning Danish restaurant Kong Hans Kælder and he was later chef at La Fontana de Trevie in Cologne and owner of la Table des Cordeliers in Condom. In 1982 he returned to Denmark and became chef at Søllerød Inn (see page 66). Later on he went to Restaurant Gammelhøj in Aarhus and established Restaurant Marie Louise in Odense. In 2008 Michel Michaud was knighted in the French order of *Mérite Agricole* for his contribution to gastronomy.

He has published numerous recipe books and received several awards, including three stars from The Michelin Guide, among others. In the following pages Michel Michaud has provided recipes that utilise traditional Danish fruit and raw produce.

poor knights with berries (arme riddere med bær)

Creating Poor knights involves toasting some old bread and spicing it up with sugar and butter, sometimes also with milk and eggs. Brioche or other bread can be used. The dish dates back to medieval times and is called Arme riddere in Denmark, Poor Knights of Windsor in England, Arme Ritter in Germany, Pain Perdu in France.

In Denmark Poor knights are enjoying a renaissance as many of the high profile restaurants are now serving the dish in various forms. Above is Michel Michaud's version.

Poor knights with berries
(Arme riddere med bær)

500 ml (16 fl oz) full-cream milk

3 tsp jasmine tea leaves (not tea bags)

5 egg yolks

75 g (3 oz) sugar

Blend of berries
300–400 g (10–14 oz) mixed fresh berries (e.g. redcurrants, strawberries and blueberries)

A little sugar

A couple of mint leaves

Arme riddere
2 raisin buns

2 whole eggs

50 ml (1⅔ fl oz) cream

1 tbsp sugar

Seeds from 2 vanilla pods

½ tsp sweet cinnamon

100 g (4 oz) butter

sugar to dust

Tea cream
Utensils: bowl, saucepan, whisk, strainer

Pour the milk and tea leaves into a bowl, bring it to the boil and boil for 2 minutes. Whip the egg yolks and the sugar until light and fluffy and then add the boiling milk though a strainer to remove leaves. Pour the mixture back into the bowl and warm it, stirring, to 90 °C (190 °F), until it curdles. The cream must not boil. Put it aside.

Blend of berries
Utensils: bowl, knife

Put the redcurrants or other berries in the freezer for 2 minutes, so that they are completely cold. Cut the strawberries into quarters and the blueberries into halves. Leave the remaining berries whole. Roll the cold redcurrants in sugar.

***Arme riddere* (Poor knights)**
Utensils: bowl, knife, pan, kitchen paper

With a fork, blend the eggs, cream, sugar, cinnamon and seeds from the vanilla pods.

Cut the buns in half and dip both sides in the egg mixture. Toast the buns in butter on both sides in a pan until they become golden. Place them on kitchen paper to absorb some of the fat and sprinkle with sugar.

To serve: Place the tea cream in a thin layer on four plates. Place a piece of bread in the middle of each plate and sprinkle the berries around it in alternating colours.

Decorate with mint leaves.

Fruit salad of rosehips and oranges

150 g (5 oz) sugar

150 ml (5 fl oz) water

24 rosehips, cut into halves, seeds removed

1 star anise

4 oranges

28 wild rose leaves

A little sugar for the rose leaves

1 egg white

Utensils: saucepan, peeling knife, knife, bowl

Boil the sugar and water. Add the rosehips and star anise to the syrup and stir. Remove the syrup from the heat and allow to cool.

Peel the oranges and remove the pith. Cut the oranges into fillets.

Glaze the wild rose leaves with egg whites and sprinkle with sugar. Blend rosehips and oranges and add a little syrup. Decorate with rosehips.

Danish wines

The Danish wine industry

" *I would like the wine to taste like the Danish summer and preferably of a Danish summer night. Light, dreamy and airy with the flavours of forest raspberries, ripe blackberries, small fine acidic forest strawberries, elderberry flowers and the irresistibly light aromatic Danish apple variety Ingrid Marie* "

Sven Moesgaard

DRIVING THROUGH THE VINEYARDS of Denmark is an extraordinary experience that unfortunately also bears witness to the effects of climate change. Danes no longer need to travel south for a wine tour; they can follow scenic routes throughout Denmark and visit Danish wine cellars. In fact, Danish sweet, sparkling, red and white wines have already won awards and trophies at major international wine competitions.

The four recognised wine regions of Denmark are Bornholm, Funen, Jutland and Zealand. The European Union has allocated 99 hectares of the overall growing quota to Denmark.

In 1993 one of the pioneers in the wine industry, Michael Gundersen, planted his first vines of the Rondo variety, a hybrid from Germany. A vineyard called the Danish Wine Center was established in Avedøre only 9 kilometres south of Copenhagen's CBD. In the same year, Danish enthusiasts created the Union of Danish Wine Growers.

In August 2000 the European Union accepted Denmark as a wine producing country for table wine only. However, in 2006 restrictions were lifted, which meant that grape varieties and vintages could now be shown on the back labels of bottles, equivalent to Vin de Pays and Indicazione Geographica Tipica (IGT). In 2006 approximately 20 Danish winemakers produced a total of 40,000 bottles. The numbers have since increased to nearly 2000 hobby winemakers and 56 commercial winemakers producing wines on 19 hectares. The growth of the industry is expected to increase rapidly, but with several relatively small-scale productions.

Skærsøgaard Vineyard is the biggest winery in Denmark and also the first registered and authorised Danish vineyard. Situated in the village of Dons in the wine region of Jutland, the vineyard lies close to lake Skærsø, after which it is named. It is owned by Sven Moesgaard, a pharmacist who makes his primary living from a large food supplements company, which he established with a business partner in 1981.

The fact that Denmark is now able to produce wines is possibly due to global warming, which has extended the growing period by three weeks over the past few decades.

'It is the cool nights of the northern hemisphere and the extra long sunny days during summer that slowly ripen the grapes and result in an abundance of aromatic fruit and a delicate acid. This is the secret of Danish wine.'

> *It is so nice if one can create something where wind, sun and the warm climate come into play. To achieve the best based on the conditions given. It is almost an artistic approach. And to me it is all about finding out how we bottle this summer*
>
> Sven Moesgaard

Moesgaard says. The potato-growing soil is thin and sandy and not irrigated, which results in the vines becoming a little stressed. The soil is dry and infertile, which forces the vines to grow root nets of approx 10–15 metres. Vines are typically grown on the southern slopes in Denmark.

Moesgaard considers himself a pioneer and was thus prepared to make a lot of mistakes along the way. Unlike French winemakers, who often have the advantage of family knowledge, he has no relatives to ask for advice because winemaking is new to Denmark, so he has had to learn from experience. Moesgaard has spent a great deal of time perfecting his wine (he has even set up a laboratory to test other winemakers' wines) and has proved that he can compete, in terms of quality, with the world's most successful traditional winemakers. Moesgaard employs four assistants at Skærsøgaard, among others the German winemaker Mathias Meimberg who has gained a lot of knowledge as a 'flying winemaker' and brings great understanding of new winemaking techniques and technical know-how to the winery.

Sven Moesgaard has 13,000 vines on 4.3 hectares consisting of 60 percent red grape varieties and 40 percent white grape varieties and the wines are all made by hand. The first vines were planted in 1998 and now annual production is 10,000 bottles a year. He grows Rondo, which belongs to the Pinot Noir family and is the most popular red wine grape crossed at Sankt Laurent in Austria. Other red varieties are Leon Millot, which is an old French hybrid, Regent, which is German and a hybrid between Chambourcin and Silvaner/Muller-Thurgau, and Cabernet Cortis, which is a hybrid between Cabernet Sauvignon and Solaris and one of the fastest ripening grape varieties.

The white varieties are Orion and Solaris from Germany, Zalas Perle from Hungary, which produces a high yield, and Madeleine Angevine – a French hybrid grown in the Loire Valley that produces aromatic wines that are popular in England. It is crossed with Traminer and Comtessa grapes.

For Denmark's first vintage of 2001 Sven Moesgaard received the first gold medal at the national wine competition for best commercial sparkling wine of the year. In the same year he also received a silver medal for his sweet wine and an award for the best rosé of the year. Since then Moesgaard has received 38 Danish wine awards and 13 international medals, among others a silver medal for his sparkling Don's Cuvée at Effervescents du Monde in 2007, 2008 and 2009 as well as a gold medal for the 2006 Gold Top red wine at MUNDUSvini in Germany. At the largest wine conference of the world, the International Wine Challenge, Skærsøgaard's sweet wine won a bronze medal in 2008 and in 2009 the international judges awarded Don's 2007 sparkling wine a silver medal with the words: 'A nose of fresh limes with firm creamy pristine toastiness. Attractive mousse. What a surprise from Denmark. Bravo!'

The Sweet Blue is produced from the grape variety Solaris and contains 11 percent alcohol. It is a very fine and delicate aromatic floral wine with a fine balance of acidity and structure. Solaris shows incredibly high sugar concentration with a thin skin and responds well to botrytis cinerea, which results in distinctive sweet wines. The Danish summer is blessed with warm hours of sunshine and long warm evenings. It causes the juice to evaporate while maintaining the fruit sugar, minerals and aroma.

2008 SWEET GOLD

Prime rosé with blackthorn and hawthorn nose, blended with mangoes and prunes. Filling and sweet with long balanced acidity and clean bright aftertaste. This wine has the same substance as Sweet Blue, but the fermentation has been stopped earlier resulting in lower alcohol (8 percent) and a higher level of sweetness. The 2008 Sweet Gold was awarded best Danish wine in 2009.

2008 SWEET BLUE

This regional wine from Jutland has been made every year since 2001 but only in small quantities, which have sold out before they have even been produced. Whole bunches of grapes are pressed at frost temperatures and fermentation is stopped at 10.5 percent alcohol. This wine has touches of citrus and mango. The sweet wines and Don's are excellent accompaniments for desserts.

The sparkling wine is called Don's after the Jutland town in which it is produced. Due to naming regulations within the EU it is not allowed to use the name Champagne because it is a French trademark. The Don's Cuvée is made using the traditional champagne method (*methode traditionelle*), which means that after the primary fermentation and bottling, a second alcoholic fermentation occurs in the bottle when stored horizontally in the cellar. The bottle fermentation process takes one-and-a-half years to fully develop the flavour. Dons Cuvée contains 11 percent alcohol and is a well-structured dry sparkling wine with ripe fruit and balanced acidity. Sven Moesgaard sent the Don's Cuvée to a blind tasting against the world's best champagnes. It got 85 out of 100 points. 'It is necessary to measure against the best in the world,' says Moesgaard.

Moesgaard and other Danish winemakers, as well as scientists from the Department of Horticulture at the Faculty of Agricultural Sciences (DJF) in the University of Aarhus, are continuing to source grape varieties suitable for growing in Denmark.

Australian wine expert Richard Smart, who consults with 24 wine growing countries, recently visited Denmark and his advice was to make more sparkling wines, including red sparkling wines, because they require low alcohol and high acidity. He also recommends continuing to try different grape varieties, because there are many varieties suitable for cool climates.

Top right, bottom left and bottom right: Images courtesy of Visit Aarhus (visitaarhus.com)

Facts about Denmark

DENMARK IS PART OF Scandinavia in Northern Europe and is bordered by the Baltic Sea and the North Sea. The total population of Denmark is 5.5 million. The largest and most densely populated area is Zealand (Sjælland), which is home to Denmark's capital Copenhagen with 1.1 million inhabitants. With a population of 238,000, Denmark's second largest city is Aarhus, located on the peninsula of Jutland (Jylland). Odense, with 158,000 inhabitants, is the third largest city and is situated on the island of Funen (Fyn). Denmark occupies 43,098 square kilometres (16,640 square miles).

The country has a coastline totalling 7314 kilometres (4,518 miles) and shares a 68-kilometre (42-mile) border with Germany. It is a distinctively low-lying country – its highest point is only 170 metres (558 feet) above sea level. The landscape is undulating and varied and the soil is characterised by fertile clay or sandy moraine.

Denmark is the world's oldest kingdom and has been under Queen Margrethe II's reign since 1972. The Danish monarchy can be traced back more than 1000 years to Gorm the Old and Harald Bluetooth (both 10th-century kings). Towards the end of the 10th century, Denmark was united into a single kingdom. It has been an independent country ever since, and is thus one of the oldest states in Europe. From the 8th–11th centuries, the Danish people were among those known as Vikings.

Denmark also includes the territories of the Faroe Islands and Greenland in the North Atlantic Ocean.

Denmark is the birthplace of some of the world's most famous philosophers, physicists and designers, including:

HANS CHRISTIAN ANDERSEN 1805–1875, author, poet and storyteller

KAREN BLIXEN 1885–1962, author writing under pen-name Isak Dinesen

NIELS BOHR 1865–1962, physicist

VICTOR BORGE 1909–2000, comedian and musician

THYCHO BRAHE 1546–1601, astronomer

POUL HENNINGSEN 1894–1967, author, architect and designer

ARNE JACOBSEN 1902–1971, architect

GEORG JENSEN 1866–1935, silversmith and designer

SØREN KIERKEGAARD 1813–1855, philosopher, theologian

VERNER PANTON 1926–1998, designer

JØRN UTZON 1918–2008, architect

HANS J WEGNER 1912–2007, designer

Appendix

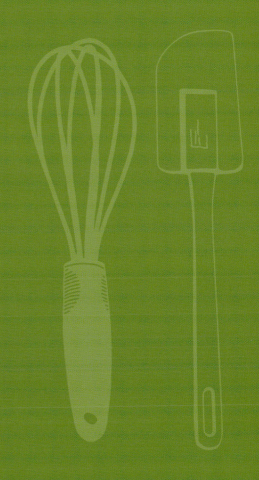

Conversions and standard measurements

LIQUID MEASUREMENTS

Tablespoons/cups	Metric/Millilitres	Imperial/Fluid Ounces (US)
1 metric teaspoon	5 ml	
1 US tablespoon	15 ml	½ fl oz
1 metric tablespoon	20 ml	⅔ fl oz
	30 ml	1 fl oz
	50 ml	1⅔ fl oz
¼ metric cup	60 ml	2 fl oz
	75 ml	3 fl oz
	90 ml	3 fl oz
	100 ml	4 fl oz
½ metric cup	125 ml	4 fl oz
	150 ml	5 fl oz (¼ pint)
	200 ml	7 fl oz
1 metric cup	250 ml	8 fl oz
	300 ml	10 fl oz (½ pint)
	400 ml	13 fl oz
	500 ml	16 fl oz (1 pint)
	600 ml	20 fl oz
	870 ml	30 fl oz
4 metric cups	1 litre	2 pints

SOLID MEASUREMENTS

Tablespoons/cups*	Metric	Imperial
1 pinch (less than ¼ tsp)	0.5 g	
1 dash (3 drops to ¼ tsp)	1.25 g	
1 metric teaspoon	5 g	¼ oz
	10 g	½ oz
1 US tablespoon	15 g	½ oz
1 metric tablespoon	20 g	¾ oz
	25 g	1 oz
2 tablespoons	30 g	1 oz
	50 g	2 oz
¼ cup	60 g	2 oz
	75 g	3 oz
	100 g	4 oz
½ cup	120 g	4 oz
	150 g	5 oz
	175 g	6 oz
	200 g	7 oz
	225 g	8 oz (½ lb)
1 cup	250 g	8 oz
	350 g	12 oz
	450 g	16 oz (1 lb)
2 cups	500 g	16 oz (1 lb)

*Note: These teaspoon, tablespoon and cup solid measurement conversions are approximations only and will vary according to the ingredients being weighed.

OVEN TEMPERATURES

Celcius	Fahrenheit	Description
120 °C	245 °F	very cool
140 °C	280 °F	very cool
150 °C	300 °F	cool
160 °C	320 °F	warm
170 °C	340 °F	warm to moderate
180 °C	350 °F	moderate
190 °C	375 °F	fairly hot
200 °C	390 °F	fairly hot
210 °C	410 °F	fairly hot
220 °C	430 °F	hot
230 °C	445 °F	very hot
240 °C	465 °F	extremely hot

Glossary

CASTOR SUGAR superfine sugar
ICING SUGAR confectioners' sugar
PLAIN FLOUR all-purpose flour
CORN FLOUR cornstarch

Useful addresses

Meyers
Kattegatvej 53
2100 Copenhagen Ø
Tel: +45 3324 3706
Email: kontakt@meyersmad.dk
www.clausmeyer.dk

Conditori & Café H.C. Andersen
Rådhusarkaden Vesterbrogade 1 B
1620 Copenhagen K
Tel: +45 3332 8098
Email: conditori@h-c-andersen.dk
www.h-c-andersen.dk

Fakkelgaarden
Fjordvejen 44
Kollund
6340 Krusaa
Tel: +45 7367 8300 Fax: +45 7367 8363
Email: info@fakkelgaarden.dk
www.fakkelgaarden.dk

Falsled Kro
Assensvej 513
Falsled
5642 Millinge
Tel: +45 6268 1111
Fax: +45 6268 1162
www.falsledkro.dk

Le Sommelier
Bredgade 63-65
1260 Copenhagen K
Tel: +45 3311 4515
Fax: +45 3311 5979
www.lesommelier.dk

Restaurant Herman
Bernstorffsgade 5
1577 Copenhagen V
Tel: +45 8870 0000
www.nimb.dk

Restaurant Frederikshøj ApS
Marselisborg Skov
Oddervej 19-21
8000 Århus C
Tel: +45 8614 2280
Email: pe@frederikshoj.com
www.frederikshoj.com

Ruths Hotel
Hans Ruths Vej 1
Gl. Skagen
9990 Skagen
Tel: +45 9844 1124
Fax: +45 9845 0875
www.ruths-hotel.dk

Saison
Strandvejen 203
2900 Hellerup
Tel: +45 39 62 21 40
Fax: +45 29 62 20 30
Email: saison@saison.dk
www.saison.dk

Skærsøgaard Vin
Nørresøvej 12
Dons, 6051 Almind.
Tel: +45 75 55 44 73
Fax: +45 75 55 44 93.
Email: info@dansk-vin.dk.
www.dansk-vin.dk

Søllerød Kro
Søllerødvej 35
3840 Holte
Tel: +45 4580 2505
Fax: +45 4580 2270
www.soelleroed-kro.dk

References

50 år med dessert – og konditorkunst by Gert Sørensen, Erhvervsskolernes Forlag, 2005.

Brændende Kærlighed by Thomas Herman, Klematis Forlag, 2007.

Dessertbogen by Gert Sørensen, Erhvervsskolernes Forlag, 1999.

Det sønderjyske kaffebord – et samspil mellem nationalpolitik og kosttradition by Inge Adriansen, Grænseforeningens Årsskrift, 1998.

Gastronomisk Leksikon by Jørgen Fakstorp & Else Marie Boyhus, Det Danske Gastronomiske Akademi og Gyldendal, 1998.

Ruths Hotel & Michel Michaud by Michel Michaud and Edit Moltke-Leth, JP/Politikens Forlagshus A/S, 2007.

Mad i Norden: Smagen af Danmark by Claus Meyer, Aschehoug Dansk Forlag A/S, 2007.

Sønderjysk Kogebog by Inge Adriansen, Christian Ejlers Forlag, 3rd edition, 1996.

Tiden på Engø Gård by Per Hallundbæk and Andreas Nordlund, Engø Gård AS, 2006.

Vin 2009 by Hugh Johnson, Politikens Forlag, 2008.

Index by recipe name

21st-century raspberry canapé (Hindbærsnitte) 61

Apple cake 88
Apple cake with syrup and cider 48
Apple soup with crisp apple rings 50
Apple with chocolate cake 100
Apples, hazelnuts and herbs 69
Aromatic dessert with flowers from the garden at Falsled Inn 77

Basic recipe (Danish pastries) 24
Black September berries with hazelnuts 78
Blue cheese from Southern Jutland and rye bread, red onion rings, gel and cress 86
Bread 'n' butter pudding with rhubarb mash 47
Bread layer cake (Brødtærte) 60
Buttermilk mousse with fresh strawberries 90

Cheese with honey 87
Cherries and chocolate cake 104
Chocolate and raspberry truffles 37
Chocolate bun (Chokoladebolle) 27
Cinnamon horn (Kanelhorn) 26
Coffee and mascarpone cake 102
Coffee bread from Fredericia (Kaffebrød som i Fredericia) 64
Cold buttermilk soup (Koldskål) 37

Danish pastries 24
Dannebrog canapé (Dannebrogsnitte) 94
Drained junket with compote of mirabelle plums and toasted oats 51

Fragilité 94
French nougat with a taste of dream cake 62
Fruit salad of rosehips and oranges 110

Gallop pretzel-shaped pastry (Galopkringle) 95
Good advice (Gode råd) 91
Goose breast (Gåsebryst) 32

Inspiration of biscuit cake (Inspiration of kiksekage) 63

Jewish cakes (Jødekager) 91
Juice blancmange with cream sauce and redcurrants 88

Lard cakes (Fedtkager) 91

Marzipan ring cakes (Kransekage) 36

Napoleon's hat (Napoleonshat) 29

Othello layer cake (Othellolagkage) 30

Passionfruit, cream chocolate and wood sorrel 71
Pears in boiled elderberries, yoghurt ice cream and nuts in vanilla 42
Poor knights (Arme riddere) 111

Raspberries with sheep's milk, red pepper and peaches 79
Raspberry, caramel and rosehips 70
Red fruit porridge (Rødgrød) with elderflower mousse 38
Red fruit pudding with milk foam and almond ice cream 54
Red porridge flavoured marshmallow cream (Rødgrød med fløde som marshmallow) 62
Rhubarb trifle 46
Rhubarb with strawberries and almonds 68
Rubinstein cake (Rubinsteinkage) 33

Sarah Bernhardt Cake (Sarah Bernhardt) 31
Sea buckthorn, carrots and crisp rye bread with liquorice 76
Snail (Snegl) 26
Soufflé pancakes with blueberries 43
Spandauer 28
Spelt rice with lemon and cherries 89
Strawberry and orange cake 103

The cake of the year 2003 with beer 39
Traditional bread layer cake from Southern Jutland 87
Traditional Danish cream cakes 29

Vanilla cream with poached blueberries and tarragon, and blood orange and passionfruit sorbet 55
Veiled farm girl (Bondepige med slør som smørrebrød) 65

Warm chocolate ganache with mazarin, rhubarb and liquorice 56

Index by category

Berry desserts
21st-century raspberry canapé (*Hindbærsnitte*) 61
Black September berries with hazelnuts 78
Buttermilk mousse with fresh strawberries 90
Chocolate and raspberry truffles 37
Juice blancmange with cream sauce and redcurrants 88
Pears in boiled elderberries, yoghurt ice cream and nuts in vanilla 42
Poor knights (*Arme riddere*) 103
Raspberries with sheep's milk, red pepper and peaches 79
Raspberry, caramel and rosehips 70
Red fruit pudding with milk foam and almond ice cream 54
Rhubarb with strawberries and almonds 68
Soufflé pancakes with blueberries 43
Vanilla cream with poached blueberries and tarragon, and blood orange and passionfruit sorbet 55

Cakes
Apple cake with syrup and cider 48
Apple with chocolate cake 100
Cherries and chocolate cake 104
Coffee and mascarpone cake 102
Strawberry and orange cake 103

Cheese
Blue cheese from Southern Jutland and rye bread, red onion rings, gel and cress 86
Cheese with honey 87

Chocolate desserts
Apple with chocolate cake 100
Cherries and chocolate cake 104
Chocolate and raspberry truffles 37
Inspiration of biscuit cake (*Inspiration of kiksekage*) 63
Lard cakes (*Fedtkager*) 91
Passionfruit, cream chocolate and wood sorrel 71
Raspberry, caramel and rosehips 70
The cake of the year 2003 with beer 39
Warm chocolate ganache with mazarin, rhubarb and liquorice 56

Compotes
Drained junket with compote of mirabelle plums and toasted oats 51
Red fruit porridge (*Rødgrød*) with elderflower mousse 38
Spelt rice with lemon and cherries 89

Cookies
Good advice (*Gode råd*) 91
Jewish cakes (*Jødekager*) 91
Lard cakes (*Fedtkager*) 91

Danish pastries
Basic recipe (Danish pastries) 24
Chocolate bun (*Chokoladebolle*) 27
Cinnamon horn (*Kanelhorn*) 26
Danish pastries 24
Gallop pretzel (*Galopkringle*) 95
Snail (*Snegl*) 26
Spandauer 28

Fruit desserts
Apple cake with syrup and cider 48
Apple soup with crisp apple rings 50
Apple with chocolate cake 100
Apples, hazelnuts and herbs 69
Cherries and chocolate cake 104
Drained junket with compote of mirabelle plums and toasted oats 51
Fruit salad of rosehips and oranges 110
Passionfruit, cream chocolate and wood sorrel 71
Pears in boiled elderberries, yoghurt ice cream and nuts in vanilla 42
Raspberries with sheep's milk, red pepper and peaches 79
Red fruit porridge (*Rødgrød*) with elderflower mousse 38
Spelt rice with lemon and cherries 89
Strawberry and orange cake 103
Vanilla cream with poached blueberries and tarragon, and blood orange and passionfruit sorbet 55

Ice cream

Apples, hazelnuts and herbs 69
Aromatic dessert with flowers from the garden
 at Falsled Inn 77
Buttermilk mousse with fresh strawberries 90
Pears in boiled elderberries, yoghurt ice cream and nuts
 in vanilla 42
Red fruit pudding with milk foam and almond ice cream 54
Sea buckthorn, carrots and crisp rye bread with liquorice 76

Macaroons

Apple cake 88
Coffee bread from Fredericia (Kaffebrød som Fredericia) 64
Rhubarb trifle 46

Mousse

Apple with chocolate cake 100
Buttermilk mousse with fresh strawberries 90
Raspberries with sheep's milk, red pepper and peaches 79
Red porridge flavoured marshmallow cream (Rødgrød med
 fløde som marshmallow) 62
Rhubarb with strawberries and almonds 68
Strawberry and orange cake 103
The cake of the year 2003 with beer 39

Nougat

Coffee bread from Fredericia (Kaffebrød som Fredericia) 64
French nougat with a taste of dream cake 62

Pancakes

Soufflé pancakes with blueberries 43

Pudding

Bread 'n' butter pudding with rhubarb mash 47

Rhubarb desserts

Bread 'n' butter pudding with rhubarb mash 47
Red fruit pudding with milk foam and almond ice cream 54
Rhubarb trifle 46
Rhubarb with strawberries and almonds 68
Warm chocolate ganache with mazarin, rhubarb
 and liquorice 56

Soups

Apple soup with crisp apple rings 50
Cold buttermilk soup (Koldskål) 37

Sorbet

Black September berries with hazelnuts 78
Raspberries with sheep's milk, red pepper and peaches 79
Raspberry, caramel and rosehips 70
Rhubarb with strawberries and almonds 68
Vanilla cream with poached blueberries and tarragon,
 and blood orange and passionfruit sorbet 55
Warm chocolate ganache with mazarin, rhubarb
 and liquorice 56

Soufflé

Black September berries with hazelnuts 78

Trifles

Apple cake 88
Rhubarb trifle 46

Traditional cakes

Bread layer cake (Brødtærte) 60
Dannebrog canapé (Dannebrogsnitte) 94
Fragilité 94
Marzipan ring cakes (Kransekage) 36
Traditional bread layer cake from Southern Jutland 87

Traditional Danish cream cakes

Goose breast (Gåsebryst) 32
Napoleon's hat (Napoleonshat) 29
Othello layer cake (Othellolagkage) 30
Poor knights (Arme riddere) 111
Rubinstein cake (Rubinsteinkage) 33
Sarah Bernhardt Cake (Sarah Bernhardt) 31
Veiled farm girl (Bondepige med slør som smørrebrød) 65

Photography credits

Casper Depka Carstens: 85

Conditori & Café H. C. Andersen: 24

Flemming Nissen: 12, 14, 22, 26, 27, 28, 29, 35, 36, 37, 38, 52, 53, 54, 55, 56, 74, 75, 76, 77, 78, 79, 82, 85, 86, 87, 88, 89, 90, 91, 92, 93, 94, 95, 120 (field)

Frederikshøj: 100, 102, 103

Gerner Jensen: 120 (mirabelle plum)

Hans Peder Sølvbjerg: 98, 99, 104

Karna Maj: 47, 57, 111

Lars Gundersen: 67

Lars Lind: 34, 39

Line Kornbeck-Mørup: 10, 23, 30, 31, 32, 33, 40, 42, 43, 60, 61, 62, 63, 64, 65, 66, 68, 69, 70, 71

Mark Morffew: 15

Ole Henriksen: 13

Ruth's Restaurant: 108, 109, 110

Saison: 41,

Skærsøgaard Vin: 114, 115, 116, 117, 118, 119

Søllerød Inn: 67

Tellus Works: 44, 45, 46, 48, 49, 50, 51

Tivoli: 58, 59

Visit Aarhus: 120 (wood, boat and seaside)

Every effort has been made to trace the original source of copyright material contained in this book. The publishers would be pleased to hear from copyright holders to rectify any errors or omissions.

The information and illustrations in this publication have been prepared and supplied by the author. While all reasonable efforts have been made to source the required information and ensure accuracy, the publishers do not, under any circumstances, accept responsibility for errors, omissions and representations express or implied.